Adversity

Creates

Purpose

Turning Pain into Prosperity

Yannik McKie

ISBN: 1548114766
ISBN-13: 9781548114763

"Photo Credit: Mark Jenkins/ My Studio Augusta"

This book was written to give honor and glory to my Lord and Savior Jesus Christ.

This book is dedicated to:

Charles and Carol Daniels, the best parents in the world! Without your enormous sacrifice, empathy, warmth, and love, I would not be the man I am today. I love you and thank you, and you have my word that I will do my best to ensure your sacrifice was not in vein.

Yannik's amazing life story has been featured on numerous media outlets including **ESPN, The Huffington Post, The 700 Club, Charisma Magazine, The New York Daily News, Good Day Atlanta**, and many more...

Adversity Creates Purpose reviews:

"Yannik's autobiography will inspire everyone... but especially teens who need a little help finding a solid path".

Chris Norwood,
Founder & Executive Director Health People, Nobel Peace Prize Nominee

"Yannik has an amazing life story! Why would a loving God allow bad things to happen to good people? Yannik McKie's Adversity Creates Purpose confronts this question with rare honesty and refreshing candor."

Thomas Settles
Fellowship of Christian Athletes Chaplain, University of Georgia

"Yannik McKie's story is a powerful testimony, made even more so by his remarkably humble and honest telling of it. Adversity Creates Purpose is an affirmation of the power of God and a revelation of how He often works in our lives. Believers will be strengthened by insights found within, while non-believers exploring the faith should take special note here... it is rare to be presented with such a clear window into the way God transforms lives".

Professor Frank Goodin
Emmy-winning Producer

"Yannik is a dynamic gentleman with an unbelievable story! In his book, Adversity Creates Purpose, Yannik uses his personal life experience to coach and counsel people through their times of grief. I highly recommend this book to anyone struggling with overcoming the pains of your past."

Todd Miller,
Founder & CEO Kolbe Academy for Servant Leadership & Adjunct Professor of Business, Houston Baptist University

TABLE OF CONTENTS

INTRODUCTION

"Yannik, are you sure that you want to share your story with the world?" I asked myself the question several times. I thought, for sure, people would judge me, and look at me differently if they knew the frightful details of my family, and of my past. There was one major factor that propelled me forward in this project. Despite my shame and embarrassment, there was planted in me the overwhelming, compelling desire to give witness to the power of Jesus Christ. Simply stated, I wrote this book because I wanted the world to know there is no adversity God cannot use for good.

In saying this, I do not mean to make light of anyone's particular situation, because there are many challenges that, at times, seem unbearable. In the present age, where we hear horrible stories of disease, frightening terrorist attacks, and massive earthquakes that ravage whole countries, it is necessary for us, now more than ever, to be reminded of God's love for us, as well as His sovereign power over our lives. I am not so arrogant as to believe that my story holds the answer to the world's despair, but, after reading an inspiring story from Phillip Yancy's bestselling book, "Where is God When it Hurts," I was confident that my story could help others who are living in a time of devastating trials.

Yancy's story took place in July of 1941 in a Nazi prison camp in Dachau, Germany. Michael Reger, a husband, father, and Christian minister, had been a Nazi prisoner for a month, and his horrific existence in this concentration camp influenced him to abandon all trust he had in a loving God. Then, in that same month of July, 1941, something happened to challenge his lack of trust. Prisoners were allowed only one letter a month, and exactly one month from the date of his incarceration, Christian Reger received the first news from his wife. The letter, carefully clipped in pieces by censors, chatted about the family and her love for him. At the bottom, was printed a reference to Bible verses: Acts 4:26-29. Reger looked up the verses, part of a speech by Peter and John, spoken after they were released from prison. "The kings of the earth take their stand, and the rulers gather together against the Lord and against his anointed One. Indeed Herod and Pontius Pilate met together with the Gentiles and the people of Israel in this city to conspire against your holy servant Jesus, whom you anointed. They did what your power and will had decided beforehand should happen. Now, Lord, consider their threats and enable your servants to speak your word with great boldness" (NIV)

That afternoon, Reger was to face interrogators, the most frightening experience in the camp. He would be called on to name fellow Christians, and if he gave in to pressures, those Christians would be captured and possibly killed. There was a good chance he would be beaten with clubs or tortured with electricity if he refused to cooperate with the interrogators. The verses meant little to him. What possible help could God be at a time like this?

As Yancy recounts the story, Reger was moved to the waiting area outside the interrogation room. He was trembling. The door opened, and a fellow minister whom Reger had never met came out. Without looking at Reger or changing the expression on his face, he walked to him, slipped something into Reger's coat pocket, and walked away. Seconds later, SS guards appeared and ushered Reger inside the room. The interrogations went well; they were surprisingly easy and involved no violence.

When Reger was returned to the barracks, he was sweating from the overwhelming tension. He breathed deeply for several moments, trying to calm himself, and then crawled into his straw covered bunk. Suddenly, he remembered the strange incident with the other minister. He reached in his pocket and pulled out a matchbox. Oh, he thought, what a kind gesture. Matches are a priceless commodity in the barracks. Inside, however, there were no matches, just a folded slip of paper. Reger unfolded the paper, and his heart pounded hard against his chest. Neatly printed on the paper was this reference: Acts 4:26-29. It was a miracle, a message from God. There was no way that minister could have seen his letter from his wife - he did not even know the minister. God arranged the event as a demonstration of His infinite power, to show he is absolutely alive, able to strengthen, and still worthy of trust.[1] God did not rescue Christian Reger from his suffering immediately, in a physical sense, but the miraculous matchbox was the small reminder he needed to restore His faith that God was still there, watching over him.. When you hear my life story, when you read my own accounting of it as it happened to me, you may find that it can be what that matchbox was to Christian Reger, a gift of hope. I know that after reading this book your physical situation may not immediately change, but like Reger your spiritual situation will, and from that changed perspective, great and positive growth can begin to take place in your life. At the crucible of pain, it may seem impossible to imagine that good can come,[2] but I have come to believe that good will come, and that God will strengthen us to bear our sufferings, if we abide in Him. What the prophet, Isaiah, proclaimed about God, over 2000 years ago still holds true today." You will keep in perfect peace him whose mind is steadfast, because he trusts in you. Trust in the LORD forever, for the LORD, the LORD, is the Rock eternal. Isaiah 26:3-4 (NIV)

THE GOOD LIFE

Sometimes, an unexpected event with dramatic distress occurs in a person's life, and as a result, that person is never the same again.[1] If I had known, at birth, the sequence of events that were to come in my life, I may have chosen to not be born.

I was born on May 5, 1978, at the South Fulton Hospital in East Point, Georgia. I was the first-born child of Lindell and Diane McKie. Two and a half years later, my little sister, Chantal, was born. Mom and Dad were both from a small town in Richland County, South Carolina, but they had big city dreams.

My father grew up in a house with extremely hard working parents. He had six brothers and one sister. My grandparents did their best to make sure all of their eight children had what they needed, but the things they wanted were left up to them to work for. My father was very well educated and graduated summa cum laude with a Master's Degree, from the University of Illinois. My Dad was always complimented on how smart he was. I would always hear stories about how he made it from kindergarten through graduate school with all A's, only making one B in his entire life! In addition to being extremely smart, Dad was also very active in school. He was the President of the, Fall 1971, "Mighty Quarter" line of the OMEGA PSI PHI FRATERNITY at his undergraduate school, Talladega College. Dad was also very cultured, with his ability to fluently speak four languages: English, German, French and Italian. He was a professor for an international training program in France for a couple of years and became quite the Renaissance man during his stay in France. He became an accomplished chef, and developed an ear for opera. As a young boy, I cringed at the sounds of opera music blaring through the walls of our house. France had such a huge impact on his life that Chantal and I were named after two of his favorite French students. My father was an ambitious, aspiring corporate executive who started out working as a flight attendant with a major airline based out of Atlanta, GA.

My mother's upbringing was a little different. Her family was smaller than my dad's; she only had three sisters and one brother. Her father was a chain smoker, as well as an alcoholic. Her mother was frustrated with everyone, and it definitely showed. My grandmother was very abusive to her children. My mom told me that my grandmother hit her with the iron, and even kicked her down the stairs. Mom would drop me and my sister off at my grandmother's apartment for the weekend. She was never abusive to us, but we hated being there because she made us eat grits for breakfast, lunch, and dinner.

The neighborhood my mom grew up in was rough. There were guys standing in the same place on the street corners all day long. I asked Mom who those guys were, and Mom, who was always honest with me, said, "Son, those guys are drug dealers." Growing up in this type of environment only made my mother want the best for Chantal and me even more. Like my dad, Mom was very smart and well educated. She was the first person in her family to graduate from college. With a degree from Winthrop she could have worked almost anywhere, but chose to stay at home to be with her kids while my father flew from state-to-state and country-to-country, making a living for us. My mother was a beautiful woman, who loved her kids.

My parents' simple upbringing made them want to show Chantal and me the best things in life. The first memories I have of my family were of our humble beginnings. We lived in a small two-bedroom apartment off Old National Highway in College Park, GA. After Chantal was born, my father received his first promotion, and we were out of that small apartment and into a nice three-bedroom home in Decatur, GA. We were moving on up!

I thought we were the perfect American family, two parents, two kids, a house, and a dog named Mickey. Family friends often joked by calling us the Cosby Family from the 1980's hit television show, "The Cosby Show."

Since my father worked for a major airline, we could fly wherever we wanted for free, and often got discounts on the finest hotels. My sister and I had the opportunity to see the world before we were teenagers. I can remember extravagant trips and cruises to the Bahamas, Bermuda, Mexico, Jamaica, Honolulu, and Waikiki. My mother loved to take these trips more than anyone; my father spoiled her, and everyone knew it. Her first name was Diane, and she was nicknamed, "Lady Di," after Princess Diana. She relished the lifestyle Dad was able to provide.

My parents did not bother with church much, but Mom made sure we attended the best private Christian schools in Georgia. I loved going to Christian school, and I loved God even more! I remember, like it was yesterday, my first grade teacher, Mrs. Sweat, told my class that Jesus loved us and died on the cross for all of our sins. She told us that we needed to ask for forgiveness for all our sins. Every night before I went to bed I said my prayers, but that particular night I remembered what Mrs. Sweat taught that day in class. I didn't just remember; I believed. And it was that day, at six years old, that the Holy Spirit convicted me and led me to accept Jesus Christ as my Savior! Getting saved at such a young age was something that I did not talk about much. I thought that people would doubt it and say, "How can you be mature enough to accept Christ as your Savior at six years old?" I realized that it wasn't because of maturity or intelligence that I made the decision to accept Christ. It was because, after I heard the truth of the Gospel spoken, the Holy Spirit used that truth to convict me of my sins and my need for God. It does not matter if you are six or sixty; the Holy Spirit has the power to lead those who are lost to Christ!

"I tell you the truth, anyone who will not receive the kingdom of God like a little child will never enter it." (Luke 18:17 NIV)

I really enjoyed my school and learning about God, but I did not stay there long. My dad received another promotion, and we had to move to Florence, Kentucky, during the middle of my second grade year. I was really upset about the move because I had a couple of really good friends, and loved my teachers. My feelings didn't matter; my dad was convinced. He was not going to miss this opportunity to climb the corporate ladder. This promotion would make him the highest ranking African American executive in the entire company!

The move to Florence, KY was a complete culture shock for me. I went from living in Decatur, GA to Florence, KY. In other words I went from being the majority to the minority. I remember our first day in Kentucky. We were unpacking our things from the car, and our neighbor's son, who was about five or six years old, was looking out his window in astonishment. As we all walked from the car to the house with our luggage, he looked at my dad and said to his dad, "Look, he is black!" He took a look at the rest of my family and became even more excited and said, "Daddy, they are all black!" My sister and I thought it was so funny. To this day I believe that we were the first black family he had ever laid eyes on. I got used to this kind of reaction towards my family; it was expected in 1986, as the only blacks living in an upper middle class area. It did not bother me much because I liked all people and could get along well with anybody. One of my best friends in Georgia was white.

My mother got my sister and me back into a good Christian school, and my dad got us into a brand new five-bedroom brick house. We liked our new school and loved our house. Mom and Dad often threw extravagant parties at the house. They became famous in the neighborhood for them. My father prepared and served some of his exquisite French dishes that made his guests' mouths water. My parents dressed my sister up in her nicest dresses and me in my best suits. Chantal and I were only about six and nine, respectively, so, of course, for a nine- year-old boy, playing dress-up wasn't much fun, but my sister loved it. My mother frequently pulled out her $10,000 fur, which I believe was just to show it off, because it wasn't that cold in the house. Our family was envied by everyone around.

My parents spent a lot of time and money living up to everyone's expectations, making sure no one was disappointed. We were living on top of the world! By this time Dad was a high level executive, and Mom was taking care of two great kids, who were honor roll students. I was playing soccer and basketball, and my sister was taking ballet and jazz classes. This was our life, and we were enjoying every minute of it! It was at this peak that our lives began to change, almost overnight.

My father had been promoted again and was put in charge of a very important program. He was given the huge responsibility of being the International Coordinator for In-Flight service; this was an important program that prepared the already 2nd largest airline in the nation, at that time, to fly into additional countries. This was very important to him, and he did not want to mess it up. My father always worked long hours, but this new project required him to work and travel even more. My father disappeared and was never at home to spend time with us anymore ... no PTA, no help with homework, and no sports games ... just work. My mother was basically a single mom with resources, who didn't have to struggle. At the time it didn't bother me and didn't seem to bother my mom either. She was very strong and could handle my sister and me without a problem. She loved the lavish life and understood that fur coats, expensive vacations, and big brick houses cost big money, so Dad had to work. Mom stayed busy shuffling me to basketball and soccer practices, and my sister to ballet and jazz lessons. We always kept Mom on the go, and she rarely complained. The only complaint she ever had was that she was tired, which was understandable.

We spent a lot of time with my dad's family in Columbia, SC. My dad had lots of siblings, which meant I had lots of cousins! We would run wild and have a ball! They were all older than I was, so I got picked on a lot. The fact that I preached to them, telling them that they will go to hell if they did not stop cursing and trying to sneak beers out of the refrigerator, only fueled the taunting. As much as I loved my cousins, I did not like spending too much time away from my parents. My father would drop me off to spend the night with my favorite aunt and uncle, but I could never make it through the entire night. My aunt and uncle always made fun of me by calling me a baby, but I did not care. I always made them take me home. For some reason I felt like I needed to spend as much time with my parents as I could.

Although my mother never said anything, I sensed other distractions that I did not understand at the time. I often had strange thoughts that there was some type of impending danger lurking. I sometimes became afraid for no reason. I had thoughts of us losing everything that God had blessed us with. But I knew God loved me, and I believed that He would protect me and my family from anything bad. We were the perfect family, living the perfect life, and I trusted God to continue to bless us.

I remember lying in the bed one night, not being able to sleep because I was having those fearful thoughts again. As I started to cry, I called for my dad. I told him I was scared and to check the garage because I didn't want anyone to break in the house to hurt us. Little did I know that what was going to hurt us was already in our home.

SOMETHING'S NOT RIGHT

It had been three years since we moved to Kentucky and about a year and a half since my dad received his last promotion. I was eleven years old, and the culture of our family had changed, tremendously. For some reason our feelings of joy and excitement turned to feelings of anxiety and uncertainty.

There were no more parties, and my dad was never at home. My mother constantly complained that she was tired and spent every second of her free time in bed. My father was gone for what seemed like months at a time. Mom frequently left Chantal and me with family and friends for weeks at a time, telling us she was going on cruises or vacations, but I knew that wasn't the whole story. My sister and I absolutely hated when Mom would leave us, and we did not understand why she would leave us so often. I knew Mom liked to travel, but even for her, these vacations seemed to be a bit much. But who was I to question it? It wasn't until Chantal and I had to move from our home in Kentucky to live with friends of the family in Memphis, Tennessee, that I knew for certain there was something terribly wrong.

Mom had gotten very sick and could not lie anymore; she said that she had a cancer-causing virus called Epstein-Barr. Whenever she claimed to be on vacation, she was actually in and out of the hospital. When Mom was hospitalized this time, the doctor said it was going to be a lengthy stay. We were told that, since Dad was still traveling around the country for work, he wouldn't be able to take care of us with Mom sick. We were so confused, but my sister and I stuck together and did not make a big deal about it. It wasn't until the day we were leaving for Memphis and stopped by the hospital to say goodbye to Mom, that we lost control.

I walked down the hall to look for my dad, and I saw him crying. I'd never seen him cry before, which confirmed that something was extremely wrong and out of his control. My father was a tough man, and I never saw any type of panic, worry or vulnerability in him before. To see my symbol of strength weakened in this way, not just with tears in his eyes, but crying as if he was in deep pain, caused me to lose it. It was as if our tears were contagious. Once my sister saw me crying, then she began to cry; and once my mother saw both of us crying, she also began to cry. With all this crying time flew by quickly, and it was time for us to leave for Memphis before we knew it.

I don't remember when we stopped crying. The last detail I remember was Chantal and me looking out the back window of the car with tears in our eyes as we pulled off, longing to turn around and go back home. We did not want to leave, especially with Mom in the hospital. This turned out to be the saddest day of my young life, but sadder days were to come. Somehow I knew my family would never be the same again.

We had to accept the truth. We were not going back home, and we were going to be in Memphis for a while, living with the Harris family. Cheryl Harris was my fifth grade teacher in Kentucky. She was the only black teacher in the school and her son and I were the only black students, so our families naturally formed a bond. Mr. Harris received a job transfer, so they'd relocated from Kentucky to Memphis. We already had a good relationship with the Harris', which made our transition a lot easier.

Mrs. Harris and her husband, Keith, had two children of their own. Their oldest was an eleven year-old son named Reggie, and his little five-year-old sister's name was Shaleah. The entire family did everything they could to make us feel at home, and it worked. Chantal and I were greatly enjoying our stay in Memphis. It had been a couple of years since she and I enjoyed any type of consistency, so it felt good to get a piece of our old lifestyle back.

I really bonded with Mrs. Harris. She was so much fun and always made me feel comfortable, resembling my mom a little. I felt like I could talk to her about anything, so I sometimes said things that I shouldn't have. I remember one day she dropped Reggie and me off at the movies, and we snuck in without paying. I thought that was so much fun, and I just had to tell somebody. So when we got back home I told Mrs. Harris what we had done, thinking that she would think it was funny, as well. Boy did that backfire! Reggie and I got in big trouble, and I learned my lesson ... to keep my big mouth shut.

Mrs. Harris was still teaching school, so I was enrolled in her seventh grade class. At twelve years old, this was my first time attending public school, and it was so cool. There was much more independence, and I took full advantage of it. I enjoyed being the class clown because it made me feel good to make other people laugh. I was happy to see others in high spirits and believed that this was a form of therapy for me. I enjoyed my stay in Memphis, but there was still a hint of sorrow that was building up on the inside of me. I just knew something wasn't right. We didn't talk to Mom and Dad much. I was told that Mom was still sick, in and out of the hospital, and Dad was still working.

One day, we were all camped around the television watching, "The Fresh Prince of Bellaire," starring Will Smith. It was our favorite TV show. Mom called us and said that she and Dad were coming in town to visit. We missed our parents so much, so we were ecstatic that we would get to see them soon. Not long afterwards, Mom and Dad arrived in town. It relaxed me to see us together as a family again. We hadn't seen them in about six months. It was nice talking and spending quality time together, just like old times.

THE TRUTH

It was about eight or nine o'clock one night, when Dad came into the living room and told Chantal and me that they needed to talk to us. We shut off the TV, got off the floor, and followed Dad into the Harris' bedroom. I immediately began to think that this is not good. My initial thoughts were of divorce. This wouldn't have been too difficult to handle, with the terrible fighting, loud cursing, and dad never being home, it was like they were divorced already. The walk from the living room to the bedroom was like walking the green mile. As we entered the bedroom, I saw Mom and Mrs. Harris sitting down and looking extremely distraught. Dad told us to take a seat on the bed. My heart was beating 1,000 beats a minute.

Dad said, "Yannik and Chantal, your mother and I are very sick. We have an HIV virus, and there is no cure." In a split second my sister and I, almost in unison, erupted into tears. I felt like I had been shot in the heart. All I could think about was everything I knew, everything I enjoyed and everything I loved was about to be taken away from me. My mind was going in a million different directions at once. How does this happen? Why does this happen? What is going to happen next? I couldn't believe that, at twelve years old, everything I loved about life was about to change.

After we cried for a few minutes things calmed down, and my dad went on to explain what an HIV virus is and how it works. He said, "HIV breaks down the T-cells in the body, which leads to another disease called AIDS. I contracted the disease, while cheating on your mother, and unknowingly passed the disease on to her." I interrupted him here and began to fire questions.

One would assume that my first question would be, "How long will you live?" Or maybe even, "How long have you known about this and kept it a secret?" It was neither of these. The first question I asked was, "Who was the woman that you cheated with?" Even though I was young, I understood the concept of risk vs. reward, extremely well. I wanted to know what woman could reward you with a gift great enough for you to risk, not only your family, but your life. I thought, "You stupid mother f…! You had a beautiful, devoted wife and two exceptional kids. What were you thinking?" I wanted him to help me understand his decisions, but unfortunately, he didn't. He told me that it wasn't important who he cheated with, and only indicated that his affair was with someone that he worked with.

My mom, my sister and Mrs. Harris were not saying much; they were just sitting there in tears. Dad continued to explain that a cure is in development, but right now the medications that are available will only slow down the dying process. He told us that their lifestyle had to change, if they were going to live long. They needed plenty of rest, lots of water and no stress. I asked him what was going to happen to him and Mom, and he said that they were not sure.

He said that for the moment Chantal and I would stay in Memphis because he was still working and traveling, when he wasn't sick in the hospital. Mom was going to stay in Atlanta to be closer to her favorite doctor, and he'll resume his residence in Kentucky. She said that the doctors in Kentucky didn't know what they were doing, but I believe the truth was that she did not want to be around my father. I did not know it at the time but Mr. and

Mrs. Harris had already been given guardianship of my sister and me.

This day helps me understand how the man from the Bible, Job, felt when he said, *"What I feared has come upon me; what I dreaded has happened to me."* (Job 3:25 NIV) I couldn't believe my life had been ruined that fast. I went from having the best mother and father in the world to what would soon be having no mother and father at all. No more parties, no more vacations, and worst of all, no more mom and dad. I was aware of human tragedies - children who died in car crashes, loving women raped and innocent people murdered - but this was different. This was my family.

I immediately began to pray. I learned in my Christian schools that God answers prayers, and my prayer was for Him to heal my parents and let them live. I also learned that prayer changes things, and I needed my family circumstances changed back to normal. I prayed everyday for a miracle and believed that the God I knew at my early age would help my family.

THE SECRET

After I survived the initial shock of both my parents being HIV positive, I tried to move on with my life. But how could I live my life to the fullest knowing that any day now, both of my parents could turn up dead? On the outside I appeared to be ok, but on the inside I was different. A cloud or a dark shadow was over me. I was not happy anymore. The things I used to enjoy did not please me as much as they used to.

I had a movie date with a friend that was preplanned for the weekend after I received the bad news. I was really excited about this date the week prior, but after finding out about my parents' sickness, I wanted to cancel it. I figured if my parents are going to die soon, I need to spend as much time with them as I can. But thank God for puberty because my hormones kicked in, and I decided to keep the date. I was twelve years old, and needless to say, I was becoming quite fond of the ladies. I had a good time!

Gratefully, my mom was still in town, so after my date I hopped in the bed with her to tell her about my night out. Yes, I was a twelve year-old momma's boy. I loved my mom and would have taken her as my girlfriend. She did everything I thought a girlfriend would do for me. She cooked, supplied my material needs and fed my ego by constantly telling me that I was smart and handsome. I can still hear her voice now, "Yannik, you can do anything you put your mind to."

My mom was my best friend. We talked and laughed all night long. It actually felt like time had reversed back to when things were normal. Maybe we both felt more relaxed because Dad had left to go back to work in Kentucky. This was the perfect opportunity for me to pry more information out of Mom. I asked her, "Do you know the lady that Daddy was cheating with?" She said, "Yannik." Whenever my mom said my first name at the beginning of her sentence, it was because she was about to say something important, and she wanted to make sure she had my attention. She said, "Yannik, your dad was not cheating with a woman. Your dad is gay."

The only thing I could do was laugh in my immaturity. Seriously? My father is gay? To a young boy, stereotypes are his reality. So my only perception of gay men was that they were very feminine and flamboyant. He was neither. My laughter fueled Mom's giggles, and we shared a hearty laugh together. Today, I praise God for the ability he gave me to find humor, even in the midst of pain. If it wasn't for that grace, I don't know if I would have made it.

After this revelation, I did not have any more questions at the moment. Mom was honest with me, and I admired her for that. At the time we had no idea that our situation would become a societal norm. Avert, a national AIDS charity, reports "In June 1981, the first cases of what is now known as AIDS were reported in the USA.[2] This means that we were among the very first American families to suffer from the deadly disease, AIDS. Years before the phenomenon of the "under cover brother," we experienced, first hand, the disastrous effects of what this secret life could do.

THE SHADOW

Mom went back to Atlanta a few days after our talk. Now it was time to focus on school and move forward. I hid my frustrations very well, but going to school made me very uneasy. I was always nervous about meeting new friends because they usually asked me why I moved to Memphis and where were my parents. These questions forced me to think about the depressing feelings I was trying to hide.

In retrospect, I cannot believe I was put right back into school without any form of professional counseling. How could anyone expect a twelve -year-old child to cope with an issue as complex as this?

I constantly felt like I had a shadow of death hanging over my life. I could never really relax, and it became harder and harder for me to focus on my schoolwork. It is hard enough for a teenager with a normal life to stay focused, so imagine a teenager with a new city, a new family and dying parents. Homework and tests were trivial in comparison.

I wondered if my schoolmates would find out that my dad was gay or that my parents were HIV positive. If they found out, would I be an outcast? HIV awareness was very low, so most people had a lot of misconceptions. Some people thought that if they were just in the same room with an HIV positive person, they could catch it like the common cold.

It was horrible living like I always had something to hide, which developed into a very bad habit of hypocrisy. I couldn't tell anyone that we were a family fighting with HIV because I would have to answer too many questions. In the past mom would tell people she had the Epstein-Barr Virus, but we decided to tell a different lie and say that she and dad were sick with cancer. Holding secrets, telling lies, and worrying about being a pariah in my own community was more than I could handle, so I did my best to ignore the truth that my life was falling apart. No one knew, including myself, the amount of pain I was feeling. I sank into a state of sadness, praying for an escape.

As I fought to keep my composure, my father was fighting to get my sister and me back home with him in Kentucky. Even though Mr. and Mrs. Harris had legal guardianship, he believed as long as he was healthy enough to take care of us, we needed to be with him. We were his kids. So he fought against my mom and the Harris' to get us back in his custody. I was so upset that dad was trying to take us from a good and stable home, only to put us back in a situation where we would not be properly taken care of.

My mother agreed with me. She did not feel like Dad was in any type of condition to properly raise two kids by himself, but Dad insisted. So instead of a long, drawn out custody battle that nobody could afford, the Harris' decided to give up guardianship and send us back to Kentucky.

UNFIT PARENT

After my sister and I moved back to Kentucky we soon realized that mom and I were right. Dad was in no condition to take care of us. He lied to everyone saying that he was doing fine, but the real truth was that he was getting weaker and weaker by the day. There were many nights that my sister had to help give my dad a bath. Our daily routine was to go to school, order take-out to be delivered for dinner, do our homework and go to bed. The house was a mess; dishes and food were everywhere.

On top of this chaos Dad tried to work, occasionally. I didn't understand why he was trying to still work in his condition. I later found out that if he didn't work his health benefits would have decreased. Without a full time job, it would have been impossible for him to find adequate and affordable health insurance, being HIV positive. But contrarily, he didn't allow his health plan to pay for all of his medications because he was afraid that someone from his job might discover his prescriptions and find out that he was HIV positive. So he paid up to $10,000 out of his pocket a month for medicine. Dad even took out a second mortgage on his home to cover some of his medical bills.

It amazes me how my father and I handled our problems in identical fashions. We were both trying to keep up this façade of having our situations all together, although this could not have been further from the truth. But, I guess, like father, like son.

Again, it was very difficult to concentrate on my schoolwork. My father's mental and physical health was worsening daily. The medicine caused Dad to be very impatient. One time my dad was checking my math homework, and he got very upset that I couldn't get two or three problems right. Instead of explaining to me how to solve the problems, he only screamed and threatened me. He told me that the next time he checked the work he was going to hit me for every problem I got wrong. That didn't make any sense to me. If he never explained to me how to solve the problems, I still wouldn't get them correct. So needless to say, I got my butt whipped that night! The medicine really got the best of him, and there were many episodes like this.

It usually takes a father a lifetime to rear his son into a great man and an asset to society. Responsible fathers teach their son how to stand up for himself, how to play sports, how to be a great student, how to understand the birds and the bees, how to treat and respect women in dating, how to pick a wonderful wife and how to provide for his family. So in my dad's defense, I believe he was very hard on me because he was trying to cram all of life's lessons in the one or two years he had left to live, which usually requires a lifetime. His goal was unrealistic and caused him to be overbearing, but I do not regret my dad's tough love because I knew his heart was in the right place. No one is perfect. It made me tougher and thorough. Today, I triple check all my work.

We had been back in Kentucky for about two months, and it was killing my mom, literally. The stress of not knowing if we were being properly cared for was taking a toll on her health. It was very important for people with HIV to stay stress free. My mom constantly called the house to check on us and tried to convince Dad to let us stay with her. She had been out the hospital for a while and was in better condition than my father. Dad really didn't want to let us go, but his main goal was to live with my mom until one of them passed away. He wanted to be happy, living as a family one last time before he died. My mother would have done anything in the world to get her children back, even grant my father's wishes.

So, she told him to send us back to Atlanta, and she would let him move in with her when he received a transfer from his job. They agreed, and my sister and I were shipped off again. We went from Atlanta to Kentucky to Memphis back to Kentucky and then back to Atlanta, all within approximately ten months. Three states and three schools in one year, but they were worth it to be back with Mom!

ONE DOWN

Mom was living in a three-bedroom apartment in Stone Mountain, GA. It felt like we were back to our humble beginnings, but I must say, it was better to be in a clean, three-bedroom apartment than a disgusting five-bedroom house. With Mom, life was almost back to normal. I was playing sports again, and my sister was back in her dance classes. My mother was one tough cookie! She even went back to school to get her Master's Degree, while she was sick. She refused to let this deadly disease stop her from living.

My dad received his transfer and was headed back to Atlanta to move in with us, or so he thought. When he showed up at the apartment, Mom wouldn't let him in. My dad had been hustled! And to this day I don't know if she had this planned from day one or if she changed her mind once he arrived. Knowing Mom, she probably had it planned from day one. I know she would have done anything to get us back, so lying wouldn't have been beneath her. After this stunt my parents didn't speak unless they had to. My dad ended up moving in with my Godfather, who also lived in Stone Mountain, but he wouldn't be there for long. Within a few months Dad moved back to South Carolina for additional family support. He spent his last days at the hospital or at his mother's house.

In the midst of all of this madness there was another problem on the rise. My mother's doctors said that Chantal and I needed to be tested for HIV because they were not positive that Mom was not infected before we were born. My mom's doctors believed that my father probably was infected with the HIV virus by a man he was sexually active with, while traveling across the world as a flight attendant or teaching classes in France, in the late seventies. Of course, I did not know it then, but the first recognized cases of AIDS occurred in the USA in the early 1980s, and it has been fiercely debated, for over twenty years, with everything from a promiscuous flight attendant to a suspect vaccine program being blamed.[1] Until this day, I don't know if that "promiscuous flight attendant" was my father or not, but it does make me wonder about how many people my father infected with HIV. I didn't let it show, but I was worried as we waited for our test results. I was already losing my parents, and I didn't want to find out that, my little sister, and I would be dying soon too. Thankfully, our results were negative. From that point on we were very careful around Mom. We wore gloves and kept everything sanitized. It felt awkward thinking twice before kissing my own mother, but it was better to be safe than sorry.

As soon as we got one victory, it seemed like we had to fight another battle. My mom's father suddenly died from a heart attack. I was not as close to my maternal grandfather as I was my paternal one, but I was still sad to see him go. My grandfather was the first person who died that was close to me. This was the beginning of me processing the feelings and emotions from death. His death was more difficult than it should have been for Mom because she felt partly responsible.

One week before my grandfather died, my mom decided to tell him the truth about her illness and how she acquired it. My grandfather had been struck by lightning twice, was an avid smoker and an alcoholic; he did not pass away until he received the tragic news about his daughter. My mom felt like her news was the straw that broke the camel's back. This additional stress was not good for Mom's health.

My grandfather's funeral was in South Carolina, and we were able to visit Dad while we were there. He did not look good at all. The side effects of the HIV fighting drug, AZT, caused his finger-nails and toenails to discolor, changing from white to a light yellow and the weight loss caused him to look anemic. This was the first time I began to feel like Dad was on his last leg. Even though my parents didn't speak much, Mom would never hesitate to let us visit Dad. But I really didn't like going. His mind and body were deteriorating, and it was really depressing to see him that way. I continued to pray for a cure, so that he would get well. But I was losing faith. The more I saw his health worsen, the more I realized that God was not answering my prayers.

Things got so bad that sometimes Dad couldn't even remember my name. One time my cousin and I visited Dad in the hospital, and he wanted me to pass him the TV remote. He looked at me and said, "Hey, uh...uh...hey, boy, pass me the remote." My cousin and I laughed about it because it was kind of funny, but it hurt at the same time. A dad that cannot remember his son's name can be disheartening.

Dad only weighed about 100 pounds; and he looked like he'd break, if hugged too hard. It was almost over, but he still fought. I believe that my father's legal will kept him fighting, which was separate from Mom's will. My dad wanted Chantal and me to live with his closest brother in South Carolina, but Mom wanted us to live in Atlanta with the Harris'. They agreed that the legal will of the person who lived the longest would be the one enforced. This was competition at its worse. Eventually, I think that my dad realized that Mom was going to outlive him and that continu-ing to fuss and fight was only prideful. I believe he accepted the fact that there was nothing more he could do in this situation and in his life.

I sensed that my dad may pass soon, so I made an effort to visit with him consistently during his last days. I remember the last conversation I had with my dad before he passed away. He apologized and said that he wished he could have done a better job. He said that he had made his peace with God, and he wanted to know if I would forgive him. I accepted his apology and gave him a hug and a kiss on the cheek. I told him that I loved him and left the hospital room, knowing that I may never talk to him again.

It warmed my heart to hear my dad say that he was sorry because until that day he hadn't said it. Although I didn't understand what it meant to truly forgive someone, I had enough love in my heart for my father to want him to die in peace. So I accepted his apology because I knew that's what he wanted hear.

Thirty-six hours after our last conversation on August 4, 1991, at the young age of forty, my father was pronounced dead.

It is unfortunate that it took death for Dad to see that he had made a mistake, or at least to admit that he had made one. God will do whatever it takes to bring us to repentance, even if that means bringing us face-to-face with death. I am sure that my father had plenty of opportunities to change his ways before he contracted HIV. But he chose to take advantage of God's grace, so God was left with no choice but to judge him for his sins.

"*Do not be deceived: God cannot be mocked. A man reaps what he sows.*" (Galatians 6:7 NIV) Unfortunately, the promiscuity my father sowed caused him to reap death. My dad had so much going for him: a great job, a large salary, and a beautiful family. But unfortunately, he let his talent and abilities take him to a place that his character couldn't keep him. A man who does not have God first in his life will eventually fall to the lusts and pleasures of this world.

"*For what is a man profited, if he shall gain the whole world, and lose his own soul?*" (Matthew 16:26 KJV) Men will spend their health gaining wealth, then pay all of their earnings to get health back.

My father's funeral was held in his hometown of Columbia, SC. It was a sad day for the McKie family and a tragedy to see a father, brother, and son taken away before his time. Dad's body was in terrible condition, so we decided to have him cremated. I believe that was the right decision, but I would've liked to have seen my father one last time.

My mother was hurting, but she refused to let anyone see it. She showed up at the funeral in a bright pink dress! My parents were not on good terms, when Dad passed. I guess this was her way of showing everyone that she was not going to mourn, and she was moving on with her life.

I sat on the front row crying because I thought that shedding a few tears was the right thing to do, as his son. The truth was that I felt relieved. I was relieved to have half of the shadow of death removed from around me. To see a grown man living in the condition of my dad's was sadder than any funeral could ever be. Watching him suffer and slowly die was torture. It was like knowing that the company you work for is downsizing, and you wake up every morning wondering if today is the day you get your pink slip. Wouldn't it be better to have gotten a release date, as opposed to living in fear everyday, wondering when the worst is going to happen? Don't get me wrong. Considering all the mistakes my father made, it still hurt to see him die; it just hurt more to see him live.

LIFE AFTER DEATH

I was glad to get some closure. After Dad died, there wasn't much of an adjustment for our family. Dad had not been healthy for years, and when he was healthy, he wasn't home much. It may seem crazy, but our life became a little more comfortable with him gone. My mother took some of my father's life insurance pay out and put money down on a nice home in Stone Mountain, GA. I loved it! It was a three-story home, and the finished basement became my own little apartment. I felt like we were moving back up. Money had gotten very tight over the last couple of years. The expensive medications combined with Mom not able to work and Dad on his last leg had drained the accounts fast!

Chantal and I were excited about our new home, and Mom was excited that she could afford to hire some permanent help around the house. She hired one of my best friend's grandmothers, her name was Ms. Kelly, and she became like family. My sister and I were thrilled about the help, as well, because it meant that we could stay involved in our extracurricular activities. Mom's health was beginning to decline, and she did not have the energy to keep up with our activities. Ms. Kelly picked us up from school, took us to any after-school activities and cooked our dinners. My mom was smart. She knew how important these after-school activities were to our well-being, and she found a way to make it happen without overextending herself.

While my sister and I were at our extracurricular activities, Mom spent time in her two support groups. It really helped Mom to be around other women who were living through the same challenges, since they were very uncommon back then. One support group was for women living with HIV or AIDS. The other support group was for women who had unknowingly married a gay or bisexual man. A decade before anyone knew what an "undercover brother" was, Mom had married and been infected by one. Nevertheless, Mom was handling her situation well, a lot better than I was.

Maybe she should have found a support group for me because I was about to lose my mind! I felt unprotected and afraid. My hope for a miracle had turned into anger. I felt like the loving God I knew had transformed into a big bully, who had decided He was going to pick on me! If my dad got infected with HIV in the late 70's or the early 80's like the doctors believed he did, according to Avert an international aids charity, he could have been one of the first 500 people in the United States diagnosed with this terrible disease. I did not believe God could have a purpose for such an awful coincidence. My earthly father let me down and my Heavenly Father let it happen. My anger at God made it hard for me to hold on to my faith and be comforted by religion.[3] I blamed all of my problems on God and my dad. I loved and trusted both of them, only to be disappointed.

How could a loving God allow this kind of tragedy? I accused Him of making a mistake. How could a caring father make such selfish decisions? As I learned more about the character of a real man and his responsibilities to his family, I hated my father for not being that man. I thought he was a stupid, selfish punk … stupid for contracting HIV, selfish for caring more about his lusts than he did his family and a punk for being homosexual. I could understand his stupidity because we all have a lapse in common sense sometimes. I could even understand his selfishness because, as human beings, it is natural for us to care more about ourselves than we do someone else. But Dad being sexually attracted to men was something I did not understand. Never in a million years would I have thought that my dad was gay. He was so tough and ambitious; there'd been no clues.

What confused me the most, as a young teenage boy, was wondering if I would be gay. I didn't know if it was hereditary. Would I just wake up one day feminine and flamboyant? I called Mrs. Harris in Memphis to ask her if I would be gay. She just laughed and said, "No baby, you won't be gay. You like girls too much!" But how could I make sure?

"Your enemy the devil prowls around like a roaring lion looking for someone to devour." (I Peter 5:8 NIV) Satan wasted no time using these fears and worries against me by casting doubt about God's love and control over my life. I'd decided that I did not need God. If He was going to let tragedies like this happen throughout my life, I could do better by myself. And that's exactly what I did ... took control of my own life and fulfilled my own desires.

The emotional stress sometimes caused my mother to rush me to the hospital for terrible migraines. I often experienced dizziness, extreme blurred vision, and unbearable nausea. The doctors ran CAT scans, gave me shots and several medications, but nothing helped. Doctor's said that during very emotional times the brain releases toxins, and these toxins can cause blood vessel changes that could cause migraines.

I was a ticking time bomb, and it did not take much to set me off. When I became angry, which was often, I kicked doors, punched walls, and threw whatever was near me. It was difficult for my mom to understand what was going on with me. She expected me to be the level-headed, responsible man of the house, which was an unfair expectation. Because of my mom's pain it was hard for her to be sympathetic to my struggles. Because of my pain it was hard for me to be sympathetic to her struggles. So we constantly had a tug-of-war for attention and comfort between us.

Since Mom and I were not seeing eye-to-eye anymore, our relationship began to diminish. Our arguments reminded Mom of her fights with Dad. Sometimes she was disgusted, when she looked at me and would say, "Just get out of my face, looking just like your daddy!" This was probably the reason I lived in the basement, so that she didn't have to see me. As my relationship with Mom declined, Chantal's relationship with her improved. All of a sudden, in my mother's eyes my sister could do no wrong. Whenever I made Mom mad, she and Chantal sat in the bed crying and talking about how much I irritated them. Whatever I did wrong was my fault, and whatever my sister did wrong was my fault. I couldn't win for losing, so I just stopped trying. It was so frustrating being the only male in the house. Nobody understood me. I really wished that my dad had been the man he was supposed to be because I needed him there. I didn't think anyone cared.

As if our lives weren't hard enough, my mother was diagnosed with cancer and had to begin chemotherapy. The chemo really took a lot out of Mom. It caused her to break out in sweats or to get so cold that she would literally wrap up in almost every blanket in the house. Both diseases had my mother taking up to thirty pills a day, and some of them were the size of horse pills. However, the HIV virus made it almost impossible for her body to fight the cancer.

Mom began to experience major changes in her physical state. She was losing her hair almost as fast as she was losing weight. It was hard for me to see such a beautiful woman break down in this way. The deterioration in Mom's looks was very difficult for her to handle. She literally spent hours in the mirror putting on makeup every time she left the house. One day I was very sick at school with a migraine. I was vomiting, and could not handle the bright lights in the classroom. Early afternoon, my principle called Mom to pick me up, but she did not show up until school was practically over. I could not believe it took her that long to get dressed.

Even though Mom was insecure at times, she did not let her insecurities stop her from doing what she needed to do. When I think about how tough my mom was, it amazes me. I know that it was only God who strengthened her to deal with the major physical and mental issues she had to consistently battle. It was enough for the average person to want to call it quits, but she never did. She continued to live strong and did her best to raise her two kids. My anger kept me from realizing how inspired I should have been by her love for us. I regret disrespecting Mom the way I did and making her last days more difficult than they had to be.

LAST BUT NOT LEAST

The last year had been a difficult one. I completed the ninth grade with a 2.0 grade point average, and it was all because of my lack of focus. I did not care about school at all. The way I saw it, the school was lucky I was even showing up.

Despite my troubles, I was still kind of excited about going to the tenth grade. This had nothing to do with school and everything to do with the girls at school. If it weren't for my hormones intensifying my love for girls, I would have probably dropped out of school with a ninth grade education. School actually became therapeutic for me. It was a chance for me to get away from my dysfunctional home life by seeing my friends, goofing off, and flirting with girls. I never had any intentions of learning anything; I was only there to have fun. For those few hours a day I was a regular teen.

I made sure that nobody knew my family situation. I enjoyed being popular, so I didn't want to become an outcast because of everything I was going through. I did my best to hide my circumstances so that I could fit in. While I was hiding the truth about my life, Mom was hiding the truth about her health. I could tell that her health was going down-hill because I recognized all of the signs from my dad. Her T-cells were at an all time low; the chemo wasn't helping, and what used to be HIV had turned into full-blown AIDS.

She must have felt death around the corner because she became extremely worried about who was going to have legal guardianship of my sister and me. Mom wanted us to stay in Atlanta. She knew that her passing would be hard enough for us to deal with without having to move, switch schools, and find new friends again. In the last three years, my sister and I had attended a total of nine different schools. Mr. and Mrs. Harris had two young kids of their own, who were still in school, and mom decided that she did not want them to have to move to Atlanta to take care of us.

Not being comfortable with what would happen to us hurt my mother more than any disease could. We were all she had left in her life, and she could not bear the thought of us not being properly taken care of.

One day Mom received a phone call from her friend, Carol Daniels, from Kentucky. Her husband, Charles, worked at the same airline that my dad did. They were good, down-to-earth people, who had grown up in South Carolina not too far from where my parents were from. My mom really respected the Daniels because of how sincere, humble and God fearing they were. One day Carol called the house but Mom was crying too hard to talk on the phone. Every once and a while the stress of fighting two diseases and raising two kids would hit mom all at once and she would go through intense crying spells. Carol said that she would call back, but before she hung up she told Mom that she would do whatever she could to help.

I am not sure what Carol meant when she offered to help, but Mom put her to the test. Mom called Carol back and asked her if she and Charles would move to Atlanta to take care of Chantal and me in the event of her death. I've heard of asking for favors, but "will you move your family to another state to take care of my ill-tempered fifteen-year-old son and my spoiled twelve-year-old daughter," is way beyond a favor. This question took a lot of courage to ask and even more courage to say yes. But that is exactly what happened!

Carol said yes without hesitation. She had not yet talked to her husband, Charles, but I guess she knew his heart. Once she mentioned it to him, he said yes just as fast as she did. They agreed to move to Atlanta with us and take legal guardianship in the event of my mom's death. This took a huge load off mom's back, but Chantal and I were not happy.

Not that there was anything wrong with the Daniels; they were fine. When we were in Kentucky, we stayed with them for about a week, one time, when Mom and Dad were in the hospital. They were very nice, but we did not know them as well as we knew the Harris family. Charles and Carol have two children, just like the Harris', except their kids were older and already in college. They were recent empty-nesters. The Harris' had kids our age; we had lived with them before for months, and they were lots of fun. But nevertheless, Mom had made her decision.

Since my mom knew her time on this earth was short, she and the Daniels began to make plans. Although I was not very excited about my new parents, I knew they were special. Who would commit to raising two kids, who had been through what we'd been through? Plus Carol had to quit her job, and Charles had to take a demotion. He was a team leader in his division at the airline and was being groomed for a promotion. Unfortunately, the airline did not have the same position available in Atlanta, so in order to get transferred, he had to take a demotion along with a pay cut.

Even to this day, their sacrifice is humbling and almost unbelievable. Some people wonder if Mom had given them money to take us in; she did not. I am not sure if the Daniels would have taken any money if it was offered. This sacrifice was about God, not about money.

With mom's health dwindling fast, they made plans for Carol to visit Atlanta soon to see how the household operated. So in December 1993, Carol came to visit us for a couple of weeks. Little did she know that a couple of weeks would turn into years. One day during Carol's stay, she took Mom to the doctor's office for a check-up. Her condition was very bad, so they admitted her back in the hospital. I knew in my heart that she may not make it back out.

I remember going to the hospital and having a talk with my mother that sounded like it could be our last conversation. Mom told me how much she loved me, to take care of my sister and how proud she was of me. When I meditate on this, it's amazing to see how much of an impact the way you live has on the way you die. My last talk with my dad was all about the past, his regrets and apologies. He took the most important time he had with me, to tell me something he could have said years before. The last talk with my mom, on the other hand, was about the future and what she wanted me to do with it. She said nothing to me about the past, only what she thought was most important for me to take into the future.

Not saying that Mom did everything right, but she did live her life to the fullest - taking care of her kids, going back to school, and never losing a bit of her "diva" attitude. It takes a strong person to motivate themselves to live life, knowing they are going to die soon. It is hard for me to get out of bed when I have a cold. I saw my mom fight cancer, HIV, and raise two kids. She did not sit around feeling sorry for herself, and she did not make excuses. When she didn't have the energy to cook, she hired a chef. When she didn't have the energy to clean, she found a maid. When she lost her hair from chemo, she bought a wig. She taught me to never sit around complaining about problems, get up, and fix them, whether you feel like it or not.

I was on Christmas break from school and spent the night with one of my good friends. His mom woke me up early on December 23, 1993 and said that I had to go home. As soon as I arrived, Charles told me "Yannik your mother passed away this morning," and even though it was expected, I took it hard. It was difficult to see such a tough women go, but no one can fight forever. Instead of that Christmas being a time of celebration for us, it was a time of mourning.

Charles came down from Kentucky to help Carol make the funeral arrangements. They did an excellent job. The service was held at our old church in Atlanta, and it was packed with family and friends. Before Mom died, she decided to be cremated, not because of her body's appearance, but because she wanted us to spread her ashes on her favorite beach in Hawaii. Even in her passing my mom was still a diva!

Walking into Mom's bedroom, I could still smell the scent of one of her favorite perfumes. It was like she was still there. It wasn't until the funeral that I actually found peace. I was so tired of seeing Mom suffer, so I was glad she was out of pain. I didn't cry because I thought it would be selfish of me to be sad, when I knew Mom was in heaven, free from all sickness and disease.

My dad brought a deadly disease in my home, used it to kill my mother and God let him do it. I didn't know if I could ever forgive them for it. My growing anger and unforgiveness were a really bad combination.

BIG ADJUSTMENT

After our mother died, Chantal and I only had about a week to grieve and get ourselves back together mentally. We were on Christmas break from school, but it was time to return. Everything in our lives always happened so fast, and it seemed like we never had a chance to truly get adjusted. Adjusting to life without Mom and Dad was not as hard as getting accustomed to life with a new mom and dad. This was one of my toughest transitions, yet.

Even though Charles and Carol are two of the nicest people on earth, I still felt like two strangers were moving into my house. From day one, I was confused. I did not even know what to call them. Should I call them by their first name, last name, or just suck it up and call them mom and dad? Did new parents mean new rules?

Charles set the tone up front, as the man of the house. He was all about tough love. Carol was the nurturer, providing unconditional love. Both were hard for me to accept but for different reasons. It had been a while since I lived with a man in the house, so it was very tough for me to accept structure and discipline from him. On the other hand, I was uncomfortable accepting motherly love from Carol because I felt like I was betraying my mom, whom I loved so much. I didn't know if I had room in my heart to love another mother.

The first time Carol dropped me off at school, I gave her a kiss on the cheek like I always gave Mom. Then I said, "I'm not going to give you a kiss everyday." She simply replied, "Ok." As if she was saying, "I hear you talking, Mr. Tough Guy, but we will see." I think Carol always knew that through my tough exterior, I was actually hurting on the inside and just needed a little love.

I tried to go back to school like nothing happened because I didn't want anybody feeling sorry for me. Again, I just wanted to be a regular teenager, but I couldn't stop getting in trouble. I was always in detention, in-school suspension, or out-of-school suspension. I was only in school to enhance my social life, not to learn anything. Although I was always in trouble, Charles and Carol were very patient with me. I believe that they were allowing me to grieve.

A few months later, I was well-adjusted to my new parents and eventually enjoyed their company. Charles played basketball with me, which my dad only did once. Carol coaxed me into deep conversations that no one else could. I had so much built-up anger and frustration that needed to be released, so I enjoyed our talks. I often joked with Carol that she was the only psychologist I knew that didn't need a Master's Degree to practice. She was so patient and understanding. She never counseled me with the typical, unsympathetic lines like, "everything happens for a reason." She knew I needed empathy and her genuine care more than I needed advice. People who are suffering don't always need a lesson in theology. They need someone to listen and tell them that it is ok to hurt and feel confused.[9]

With Charles and Carol, our lives were almost back to normal, and it felt good. I had bought my first car, and I was working a part-time job after school at Stone Mountain Park with two of my best friends. I loved to work because I loved to get paid. I had to have the newest Hilfiger, Polo, and the freshest Nikes. If I invested the same amount of energy into my schoolwork, as I did my school clothes, I could have received a scholarship to Harvard. Instead, my high school principal was threatening me with expulsion because he was fed up with my behavior.

I was never on time to class because I had three girlfriends I had to walk to their classes. When I was in class, I'd get kicked out before class was over. I was caught cheating on tests, and I just completed a suspension for throwing a chair at somebody. As far as I was concerned, this threat of expulsion was no big deal to me. I was only at this school because the basketball coach recruited me after my good performance at his summer camp. Later, I got kicked out of one of his other camps for insubordination, so my chances of making the varsity team were shot. Charles and Carol decided to transfer me to another school before I got expelled.

Overall, my relationship with Charles and Carol was pretty good, but their patience with my unruly behavior was wearing thin, especially with Charles. Who did he think he was? We could have gotten along fine, if he just went to work and minded his own business. I was sixteen years old and thought I knew everything. So we argued often. I yelled and threw things around to provoke him to hit me. It never fazed him. He would just sit there looking like: you can get as mad as you want, but I am not going to be intimidated and will stick to what is right.

Of course I didn't tell him this, but I respected him for being the man that he was. He not only told me how to be a man, he showed me. I lived in the house with Charles for years, and I never knew him to be on time for work. He was always early. I never heard him raise his voice at his wife, which is not only a testament to his character but hers also. In the twenty-two years that I've known him, I have only heard him curse once, when he fell down the stairs trying to fix a light bulb (I believe God will forgive him for that!). I did not realize how strong he was until I became an adult. At the time, though, I thought he was a fascist dictator! I couldn't wait to get out of the house to live life my way.

COLLEGE STUDENT

With Charles and I at each other's throats every day, and with trying to juggle all my girlfriends, my senior year went by quickly, and I could not have been happier. I graduated from high school in 1996 with a stellar 2.0 GPA. I did not attend my graduation ceremony. I told Charles and Carol that I wasn't marching because I did not want to wear that stupid-looking hat.

I had not taken school seriously since the fifth grade, so why in the world would I care about college? But going to the army was not an option, and neither was working full time, so I applied to college in order to get the heck out of the house. I applied to three schools: The University of Georgia, Morehouse University and Georgia Southern University. I only received an acceptance letter from Georgia Southern University in Statesboro, GA, with a few pre-acceptance requirements. I had to take remedial classes during my first semester, but I was blessed to get accepted anywhere with my GPA.

Since I liked making money, I thought a major in business with a minor in marketing might be pretty interesting. I enjoyed learning about business; it was a subject that I studied often as a child. I started reading the Wall Street Journal at age fourteen and told my mom to buy me stocks instead of video games. Mom and I took money I received from birthdays and holidays to purchase stock.

She told me to pick two companies that I wanted to invest in. I decided to purchase two blue chip stocks: Nike and Coca-Cola. These were two companies I was already tracking weekly in the newspaper, and I personally spent a lot of money on their products. So it would be great to make it all back. My first 2 stock picks turned out to be gold mines. My money compounded quickly because I reinvested all of my dividends, and the stocks split a couple of times. I made over $10,000 in profit from these stocks between the ages of fourteen and eighteen. Everyone always told me that I was smart, so I knew I had the potential to have good business intelligence. Business was the perfect major for me, if I ever decided to get serious.

As for now, my major was smoking weed, with a minor in drinking. Since I was finally out of the house, I didn't have to worry about anyone looking over my shoulder. Smoking and drinking covered up my pain and took my mind off of things.

Soelle's book, **The Suffering**, suggests that "the most important question we can ask about suffering is whom it serves. Does our suffering serve God or the devil?"[4]

Instead of trying to cover up my pain and letting Satan use it to destroy me, I should have been trying to learn from it and allowing God to use it to develop me. But my faith in God was lost. I needed answers, and the "God only let this happen to you because he knows you are strong enough to handle it" was not going to cut it. I would rather have been weak, if that meant my parents would still be alive.

My anger kept me blinded from the truth that I was being led astray, so I continued to try to fix my permanent problems with temporary solutions like drugs, alcohol and sex. The devil had convinced me that I'd struggled enough and now could do whatever I wanted to do. If anyone deserves relaxation, it's me. Shouldn't I be able to have a little fun? After all, I'm not killing anybody. It's widely known that "Satan is a liar" (John 8:44); but not only is he a liar, he is also extremely clever. He watches you, learns your weakness, and tells you lies that he knows your flesh will want to believe. Although Satan is tricky, I knew that I wasn't living right. I just decided to live satisfying my flesh rather than God's Spirit.

I was addicted to pleasure. I started my day smoking weed and ended my day smoking weed. I had a different girl for every single day of the week and two for Sundays. A lot of my sexual activity probably came from my confusion regarding my father's homosexual lifestyle. No one told me if he was always gay or if he woke up one day with attraction to men. I still wasn't sure if there was a gay gene that could have been passed down to me. I needed to talk to someone about it, but everybody in my family was just as embarrassed as I was, so the topic was swept under the rug.

I just dealt with it the best way I knew how. I played it safe and protected myself from Dad's gay gene by having sex with as many women as I could, just to make sure that I didn't wake up one morning fantasizing about men. This was the result of a teenager figuring things out on my own. No one taught me that homosexuality was a spirit of sexual perversion and that my father's actions were no different than child molestation, pornography, or my behavior of fornication. I was no better than my dad. I see now that all of my sexual activity was not protecting me from perversion, but was leading me to it.

Drugs and sex did not leave me with much time for schoolwork, so my first couple of years of school were a complete waste. At the end of my second year I didn't have half the credit hours that I should have had. If a class seemed too hard, I just dropped it. I checked each syllabus on the first day of class and only kept classes when the majority of the grade came from group assignments. I liked those classes because I simply paid someone to do my portion of the work. If I had assignments other than group work, one of my lady friends took care of that, and I was smart enough to pass most of my tests with a little studying and common sense.

I did just enough work to squeeze by, and didn't get much heat from Charles and Carol. They knew I wasn't doing my best, but since my grades were ok, they really didn't give me a hard time. Even though I was living a rebellious lifestyle, our relationship was actually better. Now that I had the freedom that I always wanted, there was no reason to argue. As far as they knew, I was just a regular college student.

BUSINESS MAN

Since I spent a lot of time and money getting high, I used my business and marketing savvy to start a business selling weed. It was a no-brainer. I knew where to buy it and who to sell it to. I had the product and the consumers; what else was there to think about? So, I decided to set up shop. At first, it just paid for my bad habits but before I knew it, I was making good money. I thought life was good. I had all the weed I wanted to smoke, plus a closet full of Air Force Ones, Air Max and Air Jordans. I had thousands of dollars worth of jewelry and every girl on campus knew my name. With the campus as my playground, I was finally able to enjoy life again.

One day I walked into class when it was half over, reeking of weed. My roommate and I had just finished smoking two blunts, and I only went to class because it was a test day. I was so high and confused, when I walked into the classroom, that I couldn't find my seat. After I finally found my seat, took my test and got ready to leave, my teacher, who was also the drug abuse professor, told me that if I ever came in her class smelling like weed again, she was going to call the police on me. From that day forward this teacher despised me. She told a young lady I was dating not to continue seeing me because I would end up in jail.

I figured if I stayed out of jail, I would eventually graduate and that was good enough for me. Even though I made money selling

weed, it wasn't exciting anymore. Although I had other hustles going on, too, I wasn't satisfied. I wanted to figure out a way to make
some real money. My greed was out of control. I loved buying
whatever I wanted, whenever I wanted. If my sneakers got scuffed,
I needed the money to buy more. If I wore a shirt once, I needed
the money so that it wouldn't be necessary to wear it twice.

All I wanted to do was get paid! I had the capitol and the
connections to make things happen. I ran the streets with connected people who knew how to get money, fast. I was attracted
to hustlers because they were broken like me. I was uncomfortable around people who never had any real problems; I considered
them soft. I hated to hear people complain about their petty little
problems. But I pretended to care because I did not want anyone to
know the truth about my situation. I did not want to hear, "Don't
worry, Yannik, everything will work out." To say that everything
will work out may be comforting to the casual bystander, but it is
an insult to the bereaved and the unfortunate.[5] "Schadenfreude"
is a German psychological term, which refers to the embarrassing
relief we feel when something bad happens to someone else and not
us - The soldier in combat who sees his friend killed twenty yards
away, while he himself is unhurt. The student that sees his class-
mate caught for cheating on a test. They don't wish their friends
ill-will, but they feel a little bit of gratitude that it happened to
someone else instead of them.[6]

I felt like this is how everyone looked at my situation; I did not
think anyone really cared. They were just happy that it was happening to me and not them.

I was angry and jealous when I saw my family and friends with
their parents, as I was a third leg tagging along with my parents off
in an urn somewhere. I had a few good friends in my life who were
really genuine with their concerns, but I was too busy in anger and
self-pity to see it. I didn't confide in them because I did not think
that someone with a "perfect life" could understand the pain I was
feeling.

This was the reason I had two sets of friends. My second set of friends had problems like I did, and I felt comfortable around them. I felt like I could relax and be myself. Two of my best friends at the time were from New York. Rashad was from queens and Brooks was from Brooklyn. We were inseparable. At this particular time we were all looking for a couple extra revenue streams, so we decided to have a brain-storming session on the most efficient way to achieve this goal. Brooks was really good at this. He was a hustler in the truest form. He had plenty of connections in the streets and never had to work a day in his life. Rahsad was more laid back than Brooks and I. He was more focused on women than anything else. He usually wasn't much help when it came to generating ideas, although he said something to me that made me think.

We were talking about our guns, and Rahsad mentioned that he sold one of his guns to a friend of his in New York because his friend could not buy a gun there. A light bulb instantly popped up over my head like in the cartoons. My marketing wheels started spinning. I asked Rahsad, "What would stop us from buying guns in Georgia and taking them to New York to sell them?" We had good connections there, so we didn't predict a problem getting rid of every gun we purchased. We agreed that we could do it. So my second business venture was established, trafficking guns. We knew we had to be very careful because the police in New York don't play, when it comes to guns, and our target consumers were no Boy Scouts.

I did my research, and oddly enough, much of our strategy wasn't even illegal. In the state of Georgia, a person can typically purchase as many guns as he wants, as long as the guns are for personal use with no intentions of selling them to anyone else at the time of purchase.

So I figured that the only way we could get caught is if the feds could prove that we had intent to sell the guns at the time of purchase, and I knew that would be difficult to prove. The only way they could prove it would be by obtaining a witness from the inside of the operation. Even if somebody cooperated with the feds, the federal guidelines that I researched stated that the maximum sentence was only thirty-six months.

I realized that this was easier than selling drugs with more profit and less jail time. It was worth the risk for a 1000% profit. We decided to keep it simple on the first run - maybe some 45's, tech 9's, and a few .22 mini revolvers. We were not positive about the demand, so we needed to test the market before we spent too much capital. I was excited about my new business, and we hit the ground running.

OUT OF CONTROL

J ust as my next illegal business plan was launched, my girlfriend, Janay, who had graduated from Georgia Southern and moved back to Atlanta, called with some life changing news. I knew what she was going to say before she even opened her mouth. Her exact words were, "Yannik" (much like my mother did when she had something very serious to say), "I am pregnant." I dropped the bag of weed I was about to smoke and said, very calmly, "Don't worry about it. We will be alright."

Janay was a sweet girl with a good family, and she was very worried about what her parents and her church members would think. I tried to put her mind at ease and told her that her church has no right to judge her. That was easy for me to say because I hadn't been to church in years. Why would I praise God for my unfair life? We both agreed that abortion was not an option. Even though I was in no position to be anyone's father, I was kind of excited that I was having a child. I loved children and to have a little me running around would be cool. I went in the next room and told my boys, who were preoccupied breaking down a pound of weed, the news. They congratulated me, and we celebrated with a few blunts that eventually put me to sleep.

The fact that I would be a father soon didn't slow me down at all; my crew was making money hand over fist. I had workers to make the drive, workers to make the sales, and no matter what guns were purchased, they would sell out in less than 48 hours. The streets were on fire when they found out what we could do. Criminals were coming out of the woodwork. I had no idea there were so many gun-toting thugs in New York City, but it was a pleasant surprise for my business.

We took orders for people who knew exactly what they wanted, and we also sold wholesale for guys who wanted to set up shop themselves. We cut our profit margin in half for guys who wanted to buy in bulk, so they would have the margins they needed to make a profit. I was in charge of most of the operation. I set the prices, organized our marketing approach, and hired our employees ... all 1099. It was running like a well oiled machine.

My only real responsibility was to ensure that orders were filled correctly and to make sure the products worked. The last thing I wanted to do was sell a drug dealer $10,000 worth of fire arms that didn't work. Since my school was in the middle of nowhere, we found open fields about an hour away from campus where I tested all the weapons. We rolled up a couple of blunts and staged a makeshift firing range.

I became proficient in some high powered machinery. M 12's, Tech 9's and AK 47's were all guns that I knew how to shoot very well. I had to explain to some of the guys on the streets how to properly use these weapons. Many of them had only seen guns like this on a video game.

This conspiracy went on fluently over the next eighteen months. I loved going to New York; it was exciting and unpredictable. There wasn't a better place to work because New York is a beautiful city. After we finished working, the trip turned into a vacation. Making in a day what typically takes someone a half year to make, the hardest job was figuring out how to spend all the money. Between all my hustles it was not unusual for me to be in the mall with over $20,000 in a book bag. The shopping sprees were endless ... diamond encrusted watches, gold chains with diamond pendants, Gucci and Fendi sweaters as well as Donna Karan jeans. I wore so much jewelry that girls would ask me if it was real diamonds, gold and platinum because they only saw that much jewelry on TV. After the shopping sprees we hit the clubs and dropped lots of money in the VIP.

The girls, in my classes, would get so excited when I made it back from my trips to New York; They would laugh and giggle as I would give them their new Gucci and Fendi purses from Manhattan. For me, the best part about having money was the ability to show love. I made sure everyone around me was comfortable. I took my boys shopping and paid bills for my lady friends. Sometimes I gave away all the profits from selling weed. It was just money, and I could make more whenever I wanted. If I had put all that negative energy into something positive, I would probably be retired by now.

This is how I dealt with my adversity. I thought that my life would improve after my parents passed away. I thought if I didn't have to see them suffer every day, that the shadow of death around me would move; then I could move on with my life. But that shadow of death moved from around me to inside of me. My life, that was full of innocence, had turned into a life full of sin and death. How did I get to this point, where risking my life for money was actually a hobby, and carrying a loaded .50 caliber desert eagle everywhere I went was normal?

I was party to things that I cannot even mention, as if I did not care about anything anymore. My crew was responsible for drug and guns trafficking up and down the east coast. I would often be in a car driving 120 miles per hour, smoking weed, with no regard for the law ... as if I wanted to go to jail. My relationship with God was almost nonexistent. My heart had become calloused, and my thoughts inconsiderate. My life was spiraling out of control.

NEXT GENERATION

Janay's pregnancy was going great, and we found out that we were having a healthy baby boy! During all of my traveling I still made time to check on my son's mother during her pregnancy and I even took a silly class with her, one weekend, on how to handle the delivery. I was trying to be as supportive as I could, but my lifestyle did not afford me many opportunities like this. Her due date was the first week of December 2001, so I made sure there was nothing on my schedule during that week. This also gave me an opportunity to slow down and rest.

December came fast. I received a phone call from my girlfriend's sister saying that Janay was in labor. Rahsad, Brooks and I threw our clothes in a bag and headed to Atlanta. We made it to the hospital around 8 p.m. on the second of December, but nothing was happening. I thought to myself, "I rushed down here for this? I am not trying to sleep in a hospital tonight." Despite my feelings, I stayed patient, and my boys and I slept on the floor. Before I knew it I was rushed into the delivery room for the birth! I am sure Janay didn't feel this way, but everything happened so fast.

On 12/03/2001 I became the father of my 6 lbs. 3 oz. son, Jahlyn Ra'sean McKie. Everything went great! Janay did an excellent job, and I was blessed with a healthy boy. It is absolutely amazing to look in the eyes of your own son. It is like looking in the mirror, except you realize that you love him more than you love yourself. I believe that even though I helped give my son life, it was my son, who God used, to help give me my life back.

My heart softened again. I began to see that I needed to change, but I didn't know how. I was so deeply involved in major criminal acts that I didn't know how to start over. People were depending on me to get certain things done, so it was impossible to just quit. Despite my lifestyle and how angry I was at God, I still knew He had power; I just didn't believe He was fair in using it. But since I had no other choice and my situation was desperate, I asked God for His help. So, frustrated and fed up with the lifestyle I was living, I got on my knees one night and prayed a very simple prayer, almost like I did as a child when I asked God to come into my heart. I said, "God, I don't know how to stop doing what I'm doing. Please help me get out of the situation I'm in, but please don't allow me to go to jail. That is all I ask." It was done. I had put my life back in God's hands.

He didn't need me to give Him my life back; God could have done whatever He wanted with my life, whenever He wanted to do it. But He will not rudely intrude into our lives; He only comes when He is sincerely invited. I didn't change my lifestyle immediately, but I began to operate differently. I had a conscience again; God was beginning to move! I didn't enjoy my activities the same way. My prayer brought life back to my Spirit that had grown so lethargic, due to my sins. I always knew that my lifestyle was wrong, but there is a difference between knowing it and admitting it. Now that I had admitted it to myself and God, I could not function with the same energy and focus, which allowed room for error.

My son's Christening was in Atlanta in spring 2002, so that weekend I decided to kill two birds with one stone and grab some guns while I was in town. I called my boy, Sydney, who I grew up with, and asked him if he wanted to make some quick money. He said, "Yes." I tried to keep certain friends away from my illegal business, but I needed more soldiers to get tasks done.

I told him that I needed him to purchase some guns for me from a pawn shop that I frequently visited. I was making that shop lots of money; and figured that as long as the same person was not buying the guns, they didn't have a problem with me bringing them customers. I told Sydney what to say, what guns to buy, and where they were located in the store. I gave him the money, and I waited outside while he completed the transaction.

It took a little longer than usual. My friend came outside to tell me that they were waiting on his background check, and it was taking a while because there was a gun show in town and the system was backed up. It made sense to me, so I grabbed some tacos to eat and continued to wait. I usually sat outside the store while the guns were being purchased, just to make sure nobody was watching or following us. Everything looked normal, so I allowed my friend to continue with the purchase. Sydney eventually came out with the boxes of guns and put them into my trunk. I had a hotel room about thirty minutes from the pawn shop. We went back there and called up some friends to come hang out that night.

I woke up the next morning after a very long night and got ready to go to my son, Jahlyn's, Christening. I let a partner of mine borrow my car the night before, so I had to wait for him to return before I could leave. I also waited on Rahsad and two other friends to meet me at the hotel. All three of these guys were Jahlyn's Godfathers, so they wanted to be at the Christening, too. I didn't feel comfortable standing in the front of the church, but I wasn't going to miss my son's Christening, so I suffered through it. The ceremony was nice, and after church we all went out to eat. After lunch I said my goodbyes to Jahlyn and Janay, so I could get back to business.

I left the guns with one of my lady friends, Amber, who came by the hotel, and she took them back to school for me. I guess I respected God enough not to roll up in the church parking lot with a trunk full of automatic weapons but didn't respect Him enough not to use them to make money. Amber knew the plan; she helped me out with business like this all of the time. I told her to drive carefully, and I'd holla at her when I got back to school.

My next order of business was to pick up my usual order of marijuana because I would have some orders to fill when I got back to Statesboro. I had a several connections in Atlanta with good prices, but I could not get in touch with anybody. I decided not to keep trying, so I picked up Rahsad from his friend's apartment, and we headed back to school.

About an hour into our drive back, I got pulled over for speeding. When I rolled down the car window, the officer said that the car smelled like we'd been smoking some type of an "illegal substance." I thought, "Of course it does, Genius. We just finished smoking it." He and his partner searched the car and only found a few roaches in the ash tray. They let us go with a warning. Rahsad and I talked about what a a close call that was. I could have been pulled over with drugs, automatic weapons, and boxes full of ammunition. God had given me plenty of opportunities like this to see how one mistake could cost me my life, but I chose to ignore all the signs.

"*For the* Lord *corrects those he loves, just as a father corrects a child in whom he delights.*" (Proverbs3:12 NLT) If I chose not to correct myself, God would be forced to use the consequences of my actions to correct me, just like He did with my father. God had been more than patient with me, but instead of doing what was right, I chose to take advantage of His grace. I had a group of close friends who robbed banks, and God even gave them several chances to make the right decision and repent before He made the decision for them. They didn't get caught until they robbed their fourth bank, and they are now serving sixty-three years in federal prison. They had three opportunities to change before their grace ran out.

I often wonder how many opportunities to change my father ignored before he contracted HIV. I am not sure what kept my father from recognizing God's grace before it was too late but for me it was my anger and unforgiveness towards God that kept me blinded. I had mistaken God's mercy and patience for me being above the law. God had to step in because He could not allow His grace to be abused; it is too valuable. My disrespect for God's grace led me into the toughest battle of my life.

THE MOLE

W e finally made it back to "the boro" (as we use to call our college town). I met Amber at her apartment to make sure everything was in order, and everything looked good. Not that I had to worry; I trusted this young lady. She was a soldier and never failed to do anything that I needed her to do, which I really liked about her. I left the guns with her and told her that I would be back in a couple of days to pick them up. She didn't mind holding the guns for me because she often held my weed at her apartment. As long as I helped her take care of her bills and was there when she needed me, we were cool. So I left. I had already organized the details for my next trip, which was in less than 48 hours.

Since I had been out of town for a couple of days, I needed to check on a few things. The next day I received a few phone calls from Amber, which wasn't unusual. She usually called if it had been a while since we spoke and/or if she thought I was with another girl. Since I was with another girl, I ignored her phone calls. I figured she just wanted me to come visit her, but I was already busy, so I did not need to answer the phone.

The next morning I woke up, smoked a little, got dressed and went to class. After class my phone rang again. My caller ID. displayed that it was Amber calling. Her constant calls were ridiculous, so I irritably picked up the phone to see what she wanted.

She sounded hysterical. "Yannik!" she said. By now I know exactly what to think anytime a woman says my first name before she starts her sentence. IT'S TROUBLE!!! She said, "They kicked in my door, and they went through my closet and found the box!" I thought, "Man, they finally got me."

I had a friend who worked at the police department in Statesboro, and he alerted me that they had been watching. I said calmly, "Don't worry about it. There wasn't that much drugs, and it wasn't bagged up." Meaning, if they found the weed and it wasn't broken down and put into bags, they couldn't prove that I had the intent to distribute. So a simple possession charge would be no big deal.

"No," she said, "not that box, the box of guns!" Now she had my attention! She said that they tried to scare her and make her answer questions. Though she'd never been in a situation like this before, she watched enough TV to know that if she asked for a lawyer, they would leave her alone. So that's what she did.

I was still pretty calm, trying to figure out what went wrong. Before I could complete my thoughts, out of nowhere two white unmarked vans swooped in on me, as I pulled into my apartment complex. I stopped the car and got out slowly. Four Alcohol Tobacco & Firearms (ATF) agents jumped out of their unmarked vans with guns drawn. They screamed at the top of their lungs, "Put your hands up and get down on the ground!"

It was like a scene from a movie; I had guns pointing at me from every direction. I thought, "All of this for me?" I was flattered, but they really could have just asked me to get in the van. I was dark skinned with corn rows in the middle of Statesboro, GA. Where the heck was I going to run? They threw me to the ground and cuffed my wrists. As I lay on the ground, two agents searched me and emptied my pockets, while the other two began to search my car.

After they finished searching me they picked me up off the ground and asked me a million questions. The most important question was: did I give someone money to buy guns? I figured somebody must have gotten arrested, questioned and told them this. How else would they know? I told them that I needed to talk with my lawyer, and they left me alone for the time being. People were out of their apartments, watching the whole scene go down and looking at me like I was a crazy gangster. This was the perfect time for me to start a career in rap music.

After they finished searching my vehicle they threw me in the van to take me to jail. An overwhelming sense of peace came over me, and I could almost hear a voice saying, "Be calm; this is what you asked of me." Then I remembered my prayer to God, asking him to help me change my life. And I thought to myself, "Wow, this was not what I was expecting, but oh well." I knew right then that my life was about to change. God was going to use my arrest to get my life back on track. This was my way out the game. Nobody would want to touch me with a ten foot pole, now that I was arrested.

While I was in the van, I could hear the ATF talking to each other on their radios, saying that Savannah, GA was where the closest federal judge was located. Since I knew Savannah was at least an hour drive, I laid my head back on the high seats of the van and went to sleep. I was at peace.

Sleeping in a van with the ATF, with my hands cuffed behind my back, is a true indication that peace definitely comes from within and not any outside circumstances. Once we arrived at the courthouse, they put me in a holding cell until a judge could see me. Locked in the holding cell, my thoughts were not about prison time, bond or who was cooperating with the feds. I was thinking about forgiveness. I was actually thinking about forgiving my father.

It was so weird. Forgiving my father was something I didn't think I would ever do. I had so much anger in my heart, and no one ever convinced me to let it go. I thought my dad was a loser. I accused him of not loving his family and being a failure as a dad.

I told myself that I would never forgive him, because no one should be that dumb and make the mistakes he did. But I was locked behind bars with a four- month-old son, guilty of the same offense I charged him with.

Although our mistakes were different, our sin was the same. We were both guilty of living a life of un-repented sin, unaware that the worst could happen. I was running the streets with my life on the line everyday, with no consideration for my family - just like he did. I thought about what my four-month-old son would think, if he were mature enough to understand the type of father I was being. My pride blinded me from the truth that I was living just like my dad. The arrest was a mirror for me to see who I had really become.

King Solomon said, "*Pride goes before destruction, a haughty spirit before a fall.*" (Proverbs 16:18 NIV) I learned a valuable lesson that day: never think that you are above making any mistake at any time. Any man left to himself is capable of the worst sin. It is only by the grace of God that everyone is not either dead or in jail.

I had no idea how heavy the grudge was until I let it go. I know I should have done it sooner, but I thought that my forgiveness meant I excused his behavior, as if it was ok. But I realized that just because I forgave a person does not mean I agree with what the person did. It just means that I understand that I'm capable of making the same mistake; therefore, I can't point my finger. If I wanted to be forgiven for the mistakes I made, I had to forgive my dad for the mistakes he made.

"*For if you forgive men when they sin against you, your heavenly Father will also forgive you.*" (Mathew 6:14 NIV) Forgiveness felt good, like a mountain had been taken off of my shoulders. I was probably the happiest man in jail! What should have been one of the most terrifying days of my life, turned out to be one of the most peaceful. The Holy Spirit took what the devil meant for evil and used it for good. Although I was behind bars, I was actually freer than I had been in the last ten years.

The judge finally called me into court and after a few questions graciously released me to pretrial supervision on a $10,000 bond. As soon as I was released, I was laser focused on figuring out what in the world went wrong, but first I had to figure out a way back to Statesboro. The ATF brought me to Savannah but did not give me a ride back to school. I roamed the streets like a homeless vagrant, trying to get some change to use a pay phone. I felt and looked like a bum; it was so embarrassing. I finally got enough change, called my roommate and waited patiently for a couple of hours until he arrived.

When we returned to Statesboro, I started my investigation. I went to check on Amber, and she told me that she noticed a white van sitting outside of her door the day after we got back from Atlanta. She said that she tried to call to let me know what was going on, but I did not answer the phone. In my pride I tried to put the blame on her, asking her why she didn't leave a message. She said in her sarcastic little voice, "Well, I wouldn't have had to leave a message, if you would have picked up the phone." I believe she knew something was wrong but she felt like I was with another girl, so she decided not to leave a message out of spite. I couldn't blame her because I was an arrogant jerk.

I didn't have time to worry about that. She just informed me that I had been under surveillance for at least two days. I thought a little harder and realized exactly what happened. The pawn shop worker must have called the ATF and delayed Sydney's gun purchase to give them the opportunity to set up surveillance on us. The ATF had been following Sydney and me since then. They must have kicked in Sydney's door and questioned him into admitting that I paid him to purchase the guns, which is how they obtained the arrest warrant for me. I immediately realized that I was followed for almost a week.

But it still didn't make total sense to me. Why didn't they wait and follow us to New York, instead of busting me when they did? This obviously meant that they did not receive the whole story from their informant. So I guess Sydney was a "good snitch;" he only told them enough to get them off his back and nothing more. They knew I gave someone money to buy guns, which is my word against his. My predicament didn't seem as bad as it looked.

News about me spread throughout the entire campus like wildfire! I was Statesboro's most wanted. The ATF conducted their investigation by showing my picture to students, asking them questions and telling them that I was dangerous. My neighbor saw them trying to break into my apartment. I didn't understand. Didn't they already do their job? Why didn't they go home? I believe they realized that the evidence they had did not give them the full picture. They followed me for almost a week, and the only thing they knew for sure was where I got my haircut and how many girls I dated. They knew that I didn't pay somebody to buy guns for them to sit in a girl's closet, but their surveillance revealed nothing more. They were searching for more evidence because they jumped the gun (excuse the pun) and showed their hand too soon.

They discovered my friend, Rahsad, from surveillance video and by interrogating students about who I was close to. They believed they had a great lead, so the ATF went on a three day search for him. He was tipped off that the ATF was looking for him, so he went into hiding, hoping everything would blow over soon. But they eventually found him. I wasn't worried about the ATF questioning him at all. He was a stand up guy. Not only was he a stand up guy, he was my best friend and my son's Godfather. There wasn't a doubt in my mind; I knew he would stand strong.

Boy was I wrong! This dude sang like Beyoncé. Rahsad told them everything. They knew where I was going, who I was going with, what guns I was buying, how much they were selling them for, and I could go on and on. They probably knew which restaurants I stopped to eat at on the way. I couldn't believe it. What kind of best friend was he? How could he be so selfish? He should have been protecting me, not throwing me under the bus. I was hurt.

Two of my best friends were cooperating with the ATF and wouldn't face any jail time as long as they were willing to testify against me. They were happy to take my money, but when they got caught, put it all on me like I held a gun to their heads and made them do it. The first thing you learn in school is not to be a tattle tale. They should have known better. So the evidence stacked against me was: the confiscated guns, two people willing to testify that I paid them to buy guns, and one witness who knew where the guns were going. Now I was really worried and even more ticked off.

I was not exactly sure how to handle this. The indictment had been filed, so all three of us were on pre-trial supervision. We couldn't talk to each other and had to stay at least 500 feet away from each other. I understood my pre-trial guidelines and also knew that we could still be under surveillance, but it was so important that I try to get Rahsad to recant his story. I finally got word to him, but he wasn't willing to withdraw his statement.

Evil thoughts were running through my head. I couldn't just let Rahsad and Sydney put everything on me. They were not innocent. It wasn't fair for them to reap the fruits and not take any of the risks associated with it. They needed to be held accountable. I began to think of ways to fix it. I still had guns, money and friends; one phone call to the right person could have taken care of everything. There were people who were afraid that if I went down, I could take them down with me. So it was easy to find help to fix a situation that could get us all in trouble. I wasn't thinking about having them killed, just a little shake-up to let them know that they should think twice before opening their mouths.

But almost as soon as these thoughts crossed my mind, I heard another voice say, "Don't panic. This is what you asked me for." God was testing me to see if I would fight this situation with the flesh or with the spirit. I had the choice to do something violent because of fear or to do nothing because of faith. I made the commitment, once and for all, to trust God to do what I asked him to do. But it was difficult to accept that having faith in God may also mean a different outcome from what I was praying for. If I was going to genuinely trust God, I had to be willing to accept the worst, if that was God's will.

I learned that true faith is not trusting God because you think he is going to give you the victory; true faith is trusting God even if it means you have to lose. I had to expect the best and prepare for the worst.

MAXIMUM SECURITY

It had been a week since my arrest, and I decided to get on with my life. I stopped smoking marijuana cold-turkey to clear my head. I was not supposed to smoke anyway under pre-trial supervision, but that may not have stopped me before, so I was very proud of myself. I went back to class because I was graduating in 2 months, amazingly. I couldn't believe after six years I was finally getting out of school. Yes!

A week later, I received a letter from school officials in my school mail box stating that I was expelled due to the investigation and violations of their campus gun policy. I had to stay 1,000 feet away from all campus property. What a blower! Six years and lots of money gone down the drain. Rahsad and Amber were expelled, as well. I didn't care about Rahsad, but I really felt bad that Amber got kicked out of school because of my ignorance. The worst thing about sin is that it will always take you farther than you wanted and hurt more people than you expected. Things couldn't possibly have gotten any worse.

On April 9, 2002, I had my first conference with a lawyer. He told me that I may be in serious trouble and quoted me an absurd price for his representation in a federal case. I was too depressed to think about much of anything, so I decided to try and cheer myself up with my favorite Teriyaki wing and chicken finger combo at a popular chicken restaurant on campus. I loved to eat and hoped it would help get me out of my depression. As I parked my car and walked towards the front of the restaurant, I felt someone staring at me, so I turned around. When I looked back, I saw a big white Ford Excursion with midnight black tinted windows. It was at the drive-thru but not pulled up to place an order.

I stood at the restaurant door and stared at the truck and even though I could not see them, I knew they were staring at me. I didn't know who it was or what was going on. I knew I probably had a few enemies, so I just stood there and prepared for what was next. Before I knew it I had a .40 Caliber in my face. "Yannik, get down!" they said. I couldn't believe it! It was the ATF again, and apparently we're on first name basis. They laid me down in front of the restaurant, cuffed me and threw me into the vehicle, again.

I asked them what was going on. They asked me if I was trying to run then said, "You failed to show up for your arraignment on April 3rd, and we have a bench warrant for your arrest." I said, "Are you kidding me? If I'm trying to run, then why am I in the same place where you locked me up the first time? This does not make sense. I did not get anything telling me to be in court!" They said, "Ok, well you can explain it to the judge." Again, there wasn't a federal judge in Statesboro, so since it was after five o'clock they put me in jail overnight and planned to take me to see a judge in the morning.

Before they turned me over they locked me in a room with the head ATF investigator. I assumed he was in charge because he was the biggest and the loudest. He looked like one of the federal agents seen on TV. He was actually kind of cool to me. I knew it wasn't personal; he was just doing his job. He gave me the spiel. He said that I needed to cooperate with them because I was up against some very serious charges, and if I didn't cooperate, I didn't stand a chance. All he wanted to know was my connection in New York. He said that he wanted me to take him where the weapons were going.

This did not surprise me at all. I figured they would try to flip me sooner or later. Rahsad's statement only gave them evidence that linked to me but not with any of the other parties involved. So if they wanted to bring indictments down on anyone else involved, they needed my assistance. What an offer! This was my chance to break free. I knew I was guilty. Everyone else looked out for themselves; and I have a four—month-old baby boy, so why shouldn't I?

Since I made a commitment to operate in faith, I had to ask myself, "If I cooperated with the ATF for immunity, would it be because I felt like God told me to cooperate or because I was afraid, and wanted the easy way out?" Honestly, I was afraid, but I knew that God did not tell me to put my crimes on someone else, so that I could get away scot-free. So I told the ATF agent that I wouldn't cooperate.

He continued pushing, which usually frustrated me, but I maintained my cool. I spent the night in jail, and the ATF picked me up the next morning. They found another federal judge that was closer than Savannah, but when we arrived, they were told that we actually needed to be in Atlanta. There was confusion about the district in which my case should be tried because they were not sure how to pinpoint where the crime actually happened. Was it where the guns were purchased or where they were taken? They decided that the crime occurred in Atlanta, so the ATF drove me four hours back to Atlanta.

I thought it was going to be a rough ride with the feds, but to my surprise it wasn't bad. They were actually pretty cool. They loosened my handcuffs a little, so that I could ride more comfortably, and they stopped at a fast food joint and got me a sandwich, chips and a drink. We also told a few jokes. They were listening to outrageously obnoxious country music, and I told them, "Look guys, I'm not going to be able to take this for four hours. Ya'll are gonna have to change that station." We all laughed.

We talked about the case a little, but no real specifics. I asked them how long they had been following me, and if they were at my son's Christening. They smiled and said, "Yeah, we were some-where close." I had to give them their credit because they were good. I was looking to see if anybody was following me, and I did not see them.

Finally, we make it back to Atlanta. It was late, and a judge wasn't available, so I spent some time at the Federal Prison in Atlanta. I wasn't sure how long I'd be there, but I was hoping to get out the next day. I had only been locked up once before for a few days in a lower security prison, but Sam Nunn was the real deal.

Word had gotten to my sister that I was going to the prison, and she thought I had to spend some major time there before my trial. She was really freaking out. She watched a TV show called, "Oz," on HBO; it was a drama series about prison and inmates who were always beaten or raped. I was not really sure what to expect, but I was not worried about any of that.

The ATF checked me in, and because no one was sure how long I'd be there, I had to take a few immunization shots. After these preliminaries, the guards took me upstairs to my cell block. My roommate was an older guy, who had been locked up about four years on gun charges. He was cool. We watched a little TV, played some cards and then I went to bed. The guards woke us up at the crack of dawn for breakfast, and shortly afterwards one of the guards told me to get my things because it was time to go. So Chantal didn't have anything to worry about; no one bothered me. I wasn't there long enough to shower.

The ATF was waiting outside to pick me up and take me to the judge for the arraignment that I previously missed. Before I was taken in to see the judge, the ATF took another crack at persuad-ing me to cooperate. I couldn't put my finger on it, but something wasn't right. They said that they sent a letter, informing me of my court date, but usually important court documents were mailed certified. I began to think that the bench warrant for my arrest was just a conspiracy by the ATF to lock me up again, as an excuse to spend more time with me and try to get my cooperation. I later discovered from my court documents that the letter concerning my arraignment was returned to them with a "no mail receptacle" stamp, dated March 28th. I was not arrested again until April 10th. I may be crazy, but I am not stupid. So I stood my ground and was sent in to see the judge for my arraignment.

This judge was serious business. She obviously had a long day, and she was already under the impression that I had missed my previous court date. I did not retain my own lawyer, so I was assigned a public defender (whom I called my public pretender). He acted confused and scared to talk to the judge, like I was his very first client. I couldn't believe he was a lawyer, scared to open his mouth. Because I missed the first arraignment the judge suggested to the ATF and my public defender that I remain locked up until my trial date. My public pretender sat there like a mute and did not say a word. I almost lost it! My incompetent public defender acted like I didn't give him a reason for not showing up. All he had to do was tell her that I did not receive the court order.

I raised my hand, as if I was in a classroom. While my public defender was talking, I cut him off with my hand raised and asked the judge if I could speak. She totally ignored me! It was unbelievable that my supervised release was about to be revoked. As the judge rapped up the case to send me back to jail until my trial, which could've been six months or longer, I told my lawyer that I needed to speak. He finally convinced the judge to let me talk.

I explained to her that I did not receive the court order and that it may have been mailed to the physical address of my apartment. But my apartment complex doesn't have mailboxes, so all of my mail should have been sent to my P.O. Box on campus. The ATF agreed that my statement was possible (probably because they knew it was a set-up), and the judge ruled to let me keep my supervised release.

I was so happy because I didn't want to spend the next six months in jail. After the judge dismissed me I met with a new pretrial supervisor, and signed all of my court documents. As I headed to the elevator, I noticed a young lady following me. I thought she was another love interest, but I found out in the elevator that she was a news reporter from a major Atlanta television station. She was interested in me, alright, because it was her job. She asked me questions about the case, but I told her that I didn't have any comments. We reached the bottom floor of the Russell B Federal Building and headed out the front Spring Street exit.

Before I knew it there was a microphone at my mouth and a television camera in my face. She must have been some kind of super hero reporter because I still don't know where she pulled that microphone from. I laughed at her powers, put my court papers in front of my face and quickly walked the other way.

The feds were trying to make this a high profile case. It turned out that the iron pipeline (gun trafficking from the south to the north) was a major problem, and they were trying to end it, using me as the example. I had called a partner of mine to pick me up, so I ran to his car and rode off.

Five minutes later both of our phones blew up! People were calling me, whom I had not talked to in years, because I was on the six o'clock news. I did not answer most of the calls, but the people I did talk to thought I was crazy for laughing on television, when I had just gotten out of prison. Even though I received a lot of calls, there was only one call that bothered me. It was from my son's mother, Janay. Before she saw me on the news I'd been able to downplay the issues, but now she knew my situation was serious. She was very upset because she thought I was going to jail and wouldn't be there for my son. All I could think to do was continue to tell her that it was no big deal and that I would be alright. She was not buying what I was selling. My case began the downfall of what little relationship we had left.

I finally made it back to Statesboro and took some time to think about what I really needed to do. My trial was due to start in August, and it was the middle of April. I did not have much time, so I packed up and moved back to Atlanta. I needed to find a lawyer and make an attempt at fighting this case.

REALITY CHECK

Before I moved back to Atlanta I needed to suck it up and call Charles and Carol to let them know what was going on. They had moved back to Kentucky a couple years ago after Chantal and I settled into college. They would want to know why I was moving back to Atlanta before I had graduated. Plus I had already been on the national news three or four times, so they would find out what was going on sooner or later anyway. This was the hardest phone call I ever had to make. Imagine having to call people who completely changed their lives for you and tell them that you had been kicked out of school and indicted on federal gun charges.

It was rough. I could tell Carol was about to cry, when I told her the news. Hoping to calm her down, I told her the same thing I told Janay - that I would be ok. Charles, on the other hand, did not cry. I think he wanted to beat me up. As hard as it was, I was glad I manned-up and told them what was going on. I would have hated for them to find out any other way, and I owed them more than that.

Now, since that was over, I needed to move back to Atlanta, but I wasn't sure where to go. I did not want to rent my own apartment and sign a lease with no guarantee of how long I would be around. On top of that my main revenue stream was gone.

Thank God, my sister was gracious enough to let me stay with her until I sorted things out. For the last three or four years we weren't getting along too well, but I believe she was worried about me and wanted to help as much as she could. She had a small two bedroom apartment in North Decatur. The surroundings were nice and quiet. It would have been absolutely perfect, if I did not have to see her goofy boyfriend walking around the apartment with his bird chest stuck out all day long. I almost handled that clown, but I kept my cool and reminded myself that I had nowhere else to go.

My first order of business was to spend some time with my son. Our relationship suffered a lot because of my immaturity, and I wanted to make it right. I was so happy to be with him. I didn't realize what I had been missing out on. He was the cutest baby boy! He had big chubby cheeks, brown skin and extra curly hair. He was already five months old, and I did not want to miss another moment. Janay dropped him off with me every morning before she went to work. Even though my relationship with Janay was not great, she never kept Jahlyn from me, and I respected her for that. Now that I began to mend my relationship with my son, I could work on the next important thing, which was fighting my case.

My Godfather, my dad's fraternity brother, who took him in when my mom wouldn't let him move back with us, connected me to one of the best lawyers in Atlanta, Dwight Thomas. Dwight was the man. He was smart, confident and very flashy. I liked his style. Dwight and I got to work right away.

The first action Dwight took was moving our trial date from August to October. Dwight then told me that if I wanted to move forward and plead not guilty, I was facing 24 – 60 months in federal prison and a $250,000 maximum fine. He explained to me that the federal system doesn't have a first offenders policy like the state. He said my sentencing guideline would be determined by a point system. Since there were so many guns on my docket and I was charged with the leadership role, if I was proven guilty he couldn't get me probation. He said that the best we could do was 24 months in prison.

All things considered that wasn't a bad deal. Since the ATF did not actually catch me selling any guns, I was only charged with two lesser d class felonies. These two charges stemmed from my code-fendants' acknowledgment that I was responsible for them purchasing the guns.

When anyone purchases a gun, they have to sign the ATF Form 4473, confirming that he/she is the actual buyer. In our case, the ATF said that the signers of form 4473 indicated that they were the actual buyers of the firearms, when in truth they were not. This was a violation of Title 18 of the United States code, sections 924 (a), (1) and (2).

I was cool with accepting one of these counts because I did ask Sydney to purchase guns for me, and even though he accepted money to do it, he was not involved in the entire operation. But Rahsad knew good and well that he was way more involved than he led on. I expressed this to Dwight, but he still insisted that with all the guns on my docket there was no way out of going to jail … other than to cooperate or be proven not guilty.

This was hard and sobering news to hear from a veteran law-yer. We both knew I was guilty, so how in the world could we prove otherwise? They had two codefendants cooperating, me on tape, and I could not produce any of the weapons that were on my docket. The prosecution was also bringing down witnesses from New York. Two guys had been arrested with guns that were traced back to me. I found this hard to believe because the serial numbers on all the guns were scratched off, but I quickly discovered that the ATF had new technology that restored scratched off serial numbers. They offered these guys a reduction on their sentence, if they testified that they bought the guns from me. This was a great deal for them because both of their charges were serious. One of the guys was arrested for robbery and the other one for a shootout in Brooklyn.

The ATF's case was air tight and got stronger by the day. Going to trial and receiving a not guilty verdict was not realistic.

Cooperating was my only other "get out of jail free" card; but as bad as I wanted out, it just wasn't in God's plan for me. My instructions from God were clear: take the charges and do not put them on anybody else. I did the crime, and if it was God's will, I was going to have to do the time.

Deep down inside, I knew this was the right thing for me to do. There was no need for me to ride to New York and get everybody arrested, when I was the ringleader and the main reason those terrible crimes happened anyway. I knew that those hustlers and drug dealers would end up in jail eventually, and the feds did not need me to do it. So Dwight told me that he would do what he could, but it wasn't looking too good. He told me that he was proud of the way I was handling the situation, and no matter what happened, we were going to handle it like men.

SABBATICAL

The next few months of my life were very different from my recent past. With the negative effects of my ignorant decisions so evident, I did not have the ambition to live my usual lifestyle. I spent most of my time reading, praying, fasting and restoring my relationship with God. I know the stereotype that every time somebody is in trouble, they claim to find God. This is oftentimes true. There are a lot of people who manipulatively run to God in their time of trouble. They hope that God will see their good actions, think that they have changed and reward them by miraculously rescuing them from their troubles.

But the problem is not running to God in your time of trouble; the problem is not being sincere when you reach Him. God will always use trouble to magnify our insufficiencies, humble us, and show how tremendous our need for him is. "for my power is made perfect in weakness" (II Corinthians 12:9 NIV) Even for an almighty God, it is extremely hard for Him to communicate to a man who feels like he has it all together. I know that God put me in my humbling situation so I would become weak, run to Him, and be made strong by His power.

Instead of questioning the man who runs to God when he's troubled, we should be questioning the man who doesn't. The man that is prideful, ignores his mistakes, and does not come to God is the real problem. If we ignore God and continue in our pride and arrogance, we need to expect nothing but destruction. (Proverbs 16:18) My father was this man: prideful, arrogant, and unwilling to admit his mistakes, which is what destroyed him. Those very same traits tried to destroy me, also. All I could do was pray that my repentance was not too late.

I searched through a box of my mother's old things and found books like, "Where is God When it Hurts?" and "When Bad Things Happen to Good People." I knew that if these books helped to strengthen my mom, they could definitely help me. I also read new books like the Battlefield of the Mind, by Joyce Meyers, which helped me to clearly recognize the war between good and evil that was waging in my head. It started to become extremely evident to me that, even though I was never infected with Aids, I still almost allowed the disease to kill me. I did not know how to handle being one of the first children in America to lose both parents to HIV. I was embarrassed, angry, and confused. I had lost both of my parents to the disease by 1994, one year before Magic Johnson went public with his infection, which is what began to raise the public's consciousness about the disease. But by then, it was too late for me; my parents had died, and I was a statistic. One American study shows that almost half of aids orphans have psychiatric problems, ranging from depression to "multiple problem behavior."[10] And even though, I was still suffering with some of these issues, I was beginning to gain a better understanding of the hurt and pain I had been wrestling with all those years. I realized that I allowed Satan to use my situation to turn me against God.

The truth really can set you free! Sounds like a cliché, but it's very true. I experienced a 180 degree turn. I rededicated my life to Christ and attended church and Bible study, faithfully. I knew that if I was going to understand the adversity I had gone through, first I needed to understand the God who allowed me to go through it. My life became normal again: no drugs, no hustling, no negative peer pressure, and less sex (come on now, Rome wasn't built in a day). I still dated a couple of girls, but it was much more toned down. Some of the girls made it real easy to cut them loose; a few of them did not want to be bothered with the new Yannik.

One weekend I picked up a lady friend from out of town. As soon as I picked her up, she was ready to party and the old Yannik would have been ready too. We would have typically had the best weed to smoke and hundreds of dollars to blow. But the new Yannik did not smoke nor did I have any extra money to spend on anything frivolous, since I was no longer hustling. Her face was priceless, when I told her this. She said, "If you don't smoke and you don't hustle, then what do you do?" Most of my lady friends only knew one side of me and enjoyed my old lifestyle more than I did. Aside from attitudes I got from my leftover groupies, I was doing pretty well.

My biggest battle was fear. I tried to remain positive, but Satan made it extremely tough for me. One article in the Atlanta Journal and Constitution (AJC) titled, "College Students Risk Future for Gun Profits" was on the front page. It quoted Rahsad saying, "I can't worry about anybody else right now. I'm just concerned with myself and how I can get out of this situation." He was really testing my patience. But I knew it was not him; it was Satan using him.

"For our struggle is not against flesh and blood, but against the rulers, against the authorities, against the powers of this dark world and against the spiritual forces of evil in the heavenly realms." (Ephesians 6:12 NIV) Satan tried to use Rahsad's influence to cause me to lose my trust in God and do something crazy. It almost worked. Flagrant disrespect like this would make anybody want to do something ungodly. I wanted my codefendants to suffer and I reconsidered cooperating with the ATF in their investigation. I was almost at my wit's end. I did not receive any support from my so-called connections in New York ... not a dime for a lawyer or even payment for the last shipment of guns. By this time everyone should have known that I wasn't cooperating, but I guess they felt like

distance was necessary. So I was left high and dry by everyone. I was upset and confused. There was nothing that I wanted more than this trial to end.

I asked God again if cooperating with the ATF was what He wanted me to do, and the answer I received was silence. Sometimes God's silence can speak louder than His words. God was confident that I knew what He wanted. Shortcuts would not bring Him any honor or glory. There was nothing left for me to do, except be still and wait on a miracle. Like Maurette Brown Clark sings, "The impossible is God's chance to work a miracle," and a miracle is exactly what it would take!

So I tried to remain positive. There were exactly 25 scriptures I quoted twice a day to help me fight the fear and depression. "*Put on the full armor of God, so that when the day of evil comes, you may be able to stand your ground, and take the helmet of salvation and the sword of the Spirit, which is the word of God.*" (Ephesians 6:13, 17 NIV) The Word of God was the only weapon I had (actually, the only weapon I had that I was supposed to use). I understood that my day of evil had come, and Satan did everything he could to take advantage of me while I was weak. Satan knew that if he could get me to act in fear instead of faith he would have stolen my most powerful weapon, and I would be finished. For the only weapon I had on my side was the power of God through faith.

"*Now faith is being sure of what we hope for and certain of what we do not see.*" (Hebrews 11:1 NIV) My faith was tested with so much negativity. Satan tried to use the TV news, the AJC, the New York Times, and my codefendants to make me feel like there was no way out. He knew that without faith all of the overwhelming evidence and propaganda would eventually cause me to take things into my own hands. I realized what was happening, so every time I had a negative thought I prayed and/or quoted scripture. With my life hanging in the balance, I chose to operate in true faith. My faith was in God to answer my prayer and rescue me, even though the odds were stacked against me.

I remained disciplined to not lose the focus I had on God. I made sure that my days were routine. I read, prayed and worked out...read, prayed and worked out. Chantal made it easy for me to focus because she was too cheap to buy cable or satellite television services (she says frugal), so there wasn't ESPN, CNN or MTV to distract me. I made a little money working part time at the post office and valet parking at night. It was a far cry from the money I was accustomed to making, but it was legal. I led this simple life for about five months.

My trial date was rapidly approaching; and there were no significant changes in the case, so Dwight and I scheduled a pre-trial conference with the prosecution. A pre-trial conference is a meeting between the defense and the prosecution, which is held before the actual trial begins. A pre-trial conference can be held for many reasons, but our reason was to try to facilitate some type of agreement on the case. But the prosecution did not compromise because their case was air tight. They only offered to compromise with my cooperation, once again. They wanted to wire me, follow me with a surveillance team and send me back to New York. In return I'd receive a reduced sentence. It was a week before my trial, and the ATF had me boxed in.

This was my last opportunity to get out of this mess, but I was more upset than I had ever been before about this offer. I told them for the third time that I was not cooperating. My attitude became very defiant because I took their persistence as disrespect. What made them think that I was a selfish punk like the other guys? I said, "I guess we are taking it to trial because I am not going to do your job for you."

It was the ATF's job to figure out who the criminals were, but they tried to use me as a shortcut to do it. Sometimes people ask me why I didn't cooperate. Suggesting that, if I was really sorry for what I did, I could have simply admitted guilt. I agree, if you are sorry then you should confess; but the selfish motive the prosecution uses to influence your confession is all wrong. How could I admit my wrong doings and let someone else take my punishment, while I walk away scot-free and totally absolved of any consequences? It's both selfish and cowardly. I was sure God didn't want me to go that route. It would have taken away my integrity and God's credit.

From the outside looking in, cooperating may have seemed like the right decision, but I don't believe a decision can be right if it is influenced by something wrong. So as hard as it was, I was determined to trust God with all my heart, even if it cost me a part of my life.

My tone and attitude towards the ATF was harsh, and things were getting heated. Dwight stepped in and straightened me out. He said in a sarcastic manner, "Boy, do you want to go to jail?" The head of the prosecution team was Assistant US Attorney, Sheila Arnum, and she was fed up also. Sheila called me arrogant and told me that I was not tough. We went back and forth at each other until there was nothing left to say. "I am going to put you in jail," she said.

The meeting was dismissed, and I left their office that Friday just as mad and frustrated as I was when I found out Rahsad was cooperating. There was nothing left for me to do except wait for my trial to begin ... ten days before the big showdown.

CHANGE OF HEART

Before my trial I spent time looking at my indictment paperwork. It said in bold black letters at the top, **"U.S.A. vs. Yannik McKie."** Wow, the entire country vs. me. There are no words to describe this feeling, and no one understands unless they have been there.

In a 1996 movie called, "Gotti," the head of a small New York mafia crew breaks a few of the old family rules and rises to become the head of the Gambino family.[7] Gotti says, "The feds are like a machine. They never run out of time or money!" I was no John Gotti, but it doesn't matter who you are. The feds' resources are limitless, and unless God is on your side when you are battling against the United States Government, you don't stand a chance.

In the beginning of this case, I thought that the last couple of weekends before the trial would be very stressful, but this was not the case. I felt very relaxed and at peace. Don't get me wrong; I did not underestimate what I was up against. God gave me the peace to deal with it. Daniel 3:17 describes how I felt through a fascinating story of three young men and a fiery furnace. At the climax they were about to be thrown into the fiery furnace by an outraged king for not bowing down to a false god. They tell the king in verse 17, "*If we are thrown into the blazing furnace, the God we serve is able to save us from it, and he will rescue us from your hand.*"

Much like these three young men, I was threatened to be thrown in a fiery furnace with nothing but God to believe in for deliverance. I was up against an outraged prosecution with evidence that I had broken the law, and they were more than ready to throw me into the federal penitentiary, which is worse than any fiery furnace. However, the hope of His deliverance is not where my peace came from.

Continue reading verse 18 of Daniel 3. The three men go on to tell the king, "*But even if He (God) does not (deliver us), we want you to know, O king, that we will not serve your gods or worship the image of gold you have set up.*" That is pure peace! My peace came from knowing that if the worst happened, and God chose not to deliver me, the fire was not enough to cause me to sin or take action that was not in God's will for my life. Peace comes from the trust, not the deliverance. I trusted God, not what I hoped He would do for me.

Satan was like that king, turning up the fire and trying to cause me to fear, so that I turn away from my trust in God. But my mind was made up. I would rather be in the fire with God than to be free without Him. This was my number one reason for not taking the ATF's offer to cooperate. I wanted people to know that I had changed, that God was real and that I truly believed He could do the impossible. I spent my entire weekend inside, thinking about these things.

Sunday came around fast, and my sister and I decided to go to church together. It was one of the last Sundays before my trial, and we needed as much prayer time as possible. Chantal and I sat in the balcony; we always liked to sit up there because it's where we used to sit with Mom. I was excited to be in church that Sunday, and we enjoyed the service. It always took a while to get back downstairs from the balcony after dismissal, so we waited patiently until the crowd died down to exit the balcony. As we walked down the stairs, my eyes made contact with someone who looked very familiar. I thought in my head, "No, it couldn't be. That would be impossible."

But after further observation I noticed that it was indeed, Sheila Arnum, the prosecuting attorney on my case. My confusion was a drastic understatement. I didn't know if I should hug her because we were at church, hit her because she was trying to lock me up, or just run because I was embarrassed. This was the person who threatened to take my life away less than 48 hours ago. I couldn't believe she was at church. I'm pretty sure she was thinking the same thing about me, "What is this evil man doing at my church?"

She waited for me at the door, as I continued to wade my way through the traffic on the balcony steps. I guess she saw the confusion on my face, so she calmly said, "It's alright, baby, you can come here." After I introduced her to my sister we began to walk and talk. She asked me why I didn't let her know that I attended that church, and my response was that she never asked me.

The next words out of her mouth were, "I can't do this to you anymore." I was not really sure what she was talking about. She said that statement as if she'd been wrestling with the decision to prosecute me for a long time. She asked me about my codefendants, if everything they said about me was true. I told her that one of my codefendants was honest, but Rahsad was more involved than he made out to be. I said, "Think about it. I am not from New York; he is." She then mentioned that she was going to call Dwight the next day. I told her thank you.

I got back in the car with Chantal, still a little bewildered, and told her what just happened. Her mouth dropped. We were both in shock. When I got home, I cried out in praise to God. I knew He was working!

I replayed the scenario in my head and meditated on what happened. I thought about what if I did not get out of the bed to go to church that morning? Or what if I went to church but rushed out rudely before the benediction? What if I had been looking in another direction and did not make eye contact with Sheila before she walked out the front door? Or what if Sheila decided to visit another church that day or go to the early morning service instead of the 12 o' clock service that I attended? As I asked myself all of these questions, I realized that I had experienced a miracle.

Without God there was no way for me to see Sheila walk out of the church at the exact same time I did, with over 5,000 members. Only God, the Lord Almighty Himself, could have organized this. A devout atheist couldn't even call it a coincidence. Someone could try to dismiss this incredible coordination of events as luck, but no one could dismiss what the Holy Spirit did inside Sheila. When she saw me at church, I would have expected her to say, "I hope you were praying hard today, because you are going to need it. See you in court!" The Holy Spirit wrestled with her about my prosecution and instantly convicted her, as soon as she laid eyes on me. I saw her anger towards me with my own eyes only 48 hours ago. Two days prior she had done everything but swear to put me under the jail. At church the Holy Spirit moved on her heart and helped to change her perception of me, immediately.

When I experience a situation like this, nobody can convince me that God doesn't exist, and that He is not active in every detail of our lives. *"The very hairs on our heads are numbered."* (Luke 12:7) If that isn't detail, I don't know what is.

FALSE HOPE

By Monday my excitement had calmed down a little. I was still anxious to see how this miracle would play out. I had not heard from Dwight, yet, and I was a little nervous. Not that I doubted Sheila's sincerity, but I just didn't understand what she could possibly do to help. I finally heard from Dwight. He said that he didn't know what happened, but Sheila and the ATF wanted to meet again. My excitement grew. He scheduled the meeting but told me that he had a previous engagement, so I would have to go alone.

When I arrived, Sheila and the ATF were already there. Sheila's attitude was a little different than it was at church on the previous Sunday. I was nervous. We talked about my case and the true involvement of my two codefendants. I told them what I told Sheila at church. I said that one of the codefendants had a lot more to do with the illegal activities than he was admitting. I don't think it was a stretch on their imagination to believe that someone would be less than honest if he knew his charge would be "excused" in exchange for his testimony.

The ATF brought out more evidence and asked me more questions about the case. I thought, "When are we going to get to the good part? The part where you guys tell me you are sorry for the inconvenience, drop the charges and I am free to go?" This part never happened, and I was getting frustrated. It seemed like they were just trying to get more information from me, and there was no indication from Sheila, at all, that she was going to help me. From what I could see we were going around in circles. They even had the nerve to ask for my cooperation again. Was this a joke? I kept my cool this time, but I was absolutely infuriated.

After what I thought was a great victory, I was back to square one. Negative thoughts swarmed my head. Could I have been wrong about Sheila? Was God toying with my emotions? Would He actually take me to a mountain top one day, only to bring me to a valley the next day? I shook hands with Sheila and the ATF at the close of the meeting and went on about my business. I was outraged, as well as confused.

I drove to Dwight's office shortly after the meeting. He was still in a meeting, so I waited outside. As soon as his meeting ended, I rushed into his office and angrily filled him in on the meeting. "Why do they keep doing this?" I said, "Why do they keep trying to get me to snitch? I told you I wasn't doing that!" He said, "Yeah, I told them not to go that route." He continued to let me vent with an odd smirk on his face, as if he knew something I didn't; but he did not say much to make me feel any better. I went home, wondering what would happen next.

PAYING IT FORWARD

Not long after I left Dwight's office, he called. He sounded more excited than I had ever heard him. He said that he talked to Sheila, and she was going to remove one of the charges off my docket and transfer it back to Rahsad's. I really didn't know what all of that meant, so he explained.

He reminded me about the federal point system and how it worked. He told me that the reason I had no option for probation, only a minimum of 24 months in prison, was because of all the guns charged to me. Each gun was worth a certain amount of points. So if Sheila removed a gun charge, it would remove a portion of the points and lower my offence level. With a lower offence level my mandatory minimum of 24 months in prison would change to 5 years probation. All I needed to do was change my plea to guilty for the other gun charge. If I pled guilty to the last charge, my trial would be canceled; and the judge would determine my sentence under the federal sentencing guidelines, which were a minimum of five years supervised release (probation) to the maximum of 60 months in federal prison.

In actuality Sheila's decision was equivalent to throwing the charge out completely because Rahsad was already cooperating and couldn't be charged for the additional weapons. So since she couldn't technically eliminate the charge, she just transferred the charge from me and gave it to Rahsad, so that neither of us could be charged for it. The ATF pleaded with Sheila not to transfer my charge, but she went against their wishes.

He said that if I decided to change my plea to guilty, then we needed to meet Sheila to sign the documents. Of course I wanted to do it. I did not stand a chance, if I went to jury trial. Once the jurors saw me on tape and in pictures with guns and listened to my codefendants say that I paid them to buy guns, it would have been a wrap. I waited for God's sign of deliverance, and this was it. Back on the mountain top again, I was disappointed with myself for doubting what God was trying to do for me.

Dwight set the appointment with Sheila, and this time our meeting went just as I hoped it would. There were no surprises. I pled guilty to the other charge, and we rescheduled the sentencing date for December 17th. Before I left the meeting Sheila told me that the judge on my case was serious business and known for handing out harsh sentences. I knew that I wasn't out of the dark yet because the judge still had the right to sentence me up to five years in prison.

My sentencing date was about two and a half months away, so in the meantime Sheila asked me to join her in our church's tutoring program to mentor underprivileged children in the Bowen Homes Project in Atlanta. I told her that I would be happy to help. How could I tell her no, especially after what she had done for me? I planned to spend the next couple of months before my sentencing date working as hard as I could for this program. I wanted Sheila to know that she would never regret the decision she made to help me. I saw Sheila often, as we both poured as much as we could into these children. I started in the program to show Sheila how much I appreciated what she did. But the more I worked in it, the more I began to love it!

We tutored the children in reading on Saturdays, visited their schools and spoke with their teachers during the week. It was our responsibility to make sure that the kids received a proper education. Most of the kids, if not all of them, lived in a home with four or five siblings, but no father figure. Fathers to children in the projects were like UFO's; children heard they exist but never saw one. With no father at home the mom or the grandmother is left with all the responsibilities. The mothers didn't have the resources to make sure their children were receiving a proper education. Most of them were on welfare with barely enough money to feed their children.

We provided food for one family. As soon as we brought in the groceries, our mentees complained that the food instantly disappeared. I found this strange; and after further investigation discovered that since the children were not sure when they would receive food again, they were taking the food and hiding it in their pockets. Unlike the suburbs where children look forward to the weekends, these children looked forward to school because they were guaranteed two good meals a day. Some of the children became more and more depressed as Friday approached because on the weekend a good meal was no guarantee.

One of my mentees lived with his grandmother, who was drunk most of the time, and chased men the rest of the time. In the projects grandmothers are in their thirties, so they are not your traditional granny. Her daughter, his mother, lived under a bridge about 2 miles from the projects, and he had to see her on his way to school everyday.

I knew the children struggled with accepting their lot in life, and they needed me. The pain I endured helped to create a passion in me for children in difficult circumstances, and I quickly grew attached to them. I understood their frustration with life and knew that, if somebody did not intervene, they would head down the same path of destruction I did. Although our problems were different, they were the same. We both came from broken homes and did not understand why things had to be so tough; the gravitation towards each other was natural because we both felt the realness.

It was not always easy getting them to open up. Their hearts had grown hard from the pain, and I understood that. I did not always want the help that was offered to me at that age, so that's why I did not give them a choice. I did everything I could to make them open up, and eventually they did. These kids were very smart, street savvy and could sniff out a fake in a minute, so I believe they wanted to make sure I was genuine. The children saw people come to help all the time, but after their emotion and excitement of starting something new disappeared, so did they. Having dealt with similar issues, I understood their hesitation; and I also understood that, if I really wanted to make a difference in their lives, I had to sacrifice.

After we gained the children's trust, Sheila and I became a great team, and now I began to use my business savvy for good. We quickly formed strong relationships in several of the schools in the city, we organized volunteers, and we both visited the students, teachers, and principles almost daily. We also picked up some of the students for the weekend to stay in our homes. We fed them, clothed them and took them to church. They loved getting out of the projects, eating a good meal and receiving a good night's rest. When I drove into the projects, all the children ran towards my car saying, "Mr. Yannik! Mr. Yannik! When are you going to come and pick me up?" I enjoyed seeing the excitement in their eyes, when I went to check on them. God used this ministry to help me understand that my adversity had a purpose, and it wasn't some random act of bad luck. God taught me that, even in disorder, there can be order.

JUDGEMENT DAY

Spending time with the children really made the couple of months before my sentencing date fly by. Before I knew it, the time to see the judge had arrived. Charles and Carol flew in from Kentucky for the sentencing. It had been a couple of years since I saw them, so I was happy they were there. My son and his mother, my sister, and most of the friends I had left were there. Dwight and I had already prepared for this day, so we only met briefly before we entered the courtroom.

I was anxious, as I walked into the courtroom. We patiently waited for the introduction of the judge. She walked in soon, and everyone rose. The judge was a younger lady with a petite frame. If I had to guess, she was probably in her forties and maybe 5'5", 140 lbs. It was peculiar to see a small woman that humble and modest with so much power in her hands. Once she told us to be seated, she gave the prosecution (Sheila) her opportunity to prosecute. Sheila was expected to present the evidence and tell the judge why I should go to jail. After all, the guilty plea was in, and the charges were serious. She had already done everything she could for me, and I could not have been mad at her for doing what her job required. I knew she wouldn't suggest the maximum sentence of five years, but I certainly didn't expect what came next.

Sheila defended me! She told the judge with no inhibitions, shame or reservations, "I do not believe Yannik needs to go to jail." She explained the hardships and troubles I had been through and the amount of help I gave her with the mentoring program. It was dead silent after Sheila finished speaking. It was so shocking to see a prosecutor in her position do that. It even caught Dwight off guard, and he is never at a loss for words.

Sheila did such a good job of defending me that when it was Dwight's turn to speak all he needed to say was, "I acquiesce to the prosecution's argument." Everyone smiled; everyone except the ATF, of course. They were not happy campers. This was a high profile case, on which the ATF spent a lot of time, money, and other resources to obtain a conviction. They didn't want anything less than years of jail time for me, so, to sit through the sentencing was torture for them.

It was my turn to speak. I knew the judge had heard it all before and knew better than anyone in the room that talk was cheap. So I wanted to keep it short. I simply told her that I was wrong and made a lot of mistakes, but if given the chance for freedom, I would not mess it up. She said ok, and told me to be seated, while I awaited my sentence. My moment of truth was only minutes ahead of me. The detrimental choices I made brought me to the point where I no longer deserved to be free and my freedom would be decided by a stranger.

The judge pronounced my sentence, in what felt like slow motion, of five years probation! The courtroom erupted in cheers! I smiled, jumped up, and hugged Dwight. I walked out of the courtroom that day different than I walked in. I should have been in prison for years, but I was free. I was honored by Sheila's heroic bravery, and humbled by the judge's gracious ruling.

I hugged Charles and Carol with a new appreciation for both of them. I held my son tight with a new respect for fatherhood and what it means. I smiled at the ATF, as they walked down the hall.

One of the nicer ones smiled back and said, "Ok man, stay out of trouble!" It was a great day and a great victory!

As I walked out of the Russell B Federal Building and on to Spring Street, I somehow ended up alone. I looked up and saw my Godbrother, Thomas, standing near my car. He was at the sentencing, but we really didn't get a chance to speak because of all the commotion. I made my way closer to him. I looked him in his eyes, smiled and shook his hand. He put his hand on my shoulder, and we bowed our heads, as he led us in a thankful word of prayer. What a perfect ending to an unbelievable story, and the heartening beginning of a new one.

Even though He did not have to, God used this situation to show me that He still cared. This miracle renewed my appreciation for God and gave me a fresh outlook on life. I looked back in amazement at God's total control of my situation:

1. The day I could not find my marijuana connection, I didn't know I was being followed by the ATF. If I had found my connection and purchased, the ATF would have caught me red-handed on videotape, drug trafficking, which would have added additional points to my docket.

2. If Sydney did not tell the ATF that I paid him to buy guns, they would not have had enough evidence for an arrest warrant. This would have forced them to continue their surveillance, and in 48 hours I would have been back in New York. The ATF could have our workers on tape making hand-to-hand gun sales. I could have been convicted of gun trafficking charges in every state that we traveled through with the guns. These charges would have demanded a minimum prison sentence of over thirty years, and I would still be in jail today.

3. If the arraignment judge would have held me until my trial date, which she had the right to do, I would not have had the opportunity to speak with Sheila about my case after church.

When I thought that God was not in control of my life, I couldn't have been farther from the truth. I should have never doubted God's love for me. My pain from my parents' deaths was like a tree blocking my view of a beautiful forest. Pain is like standing very close to a large object; all you can see is the object. Only by stepping back, can the scenery around it also be seen.[8] I needed to step back from my pain and see that my life was still blessed.

In the last nine months, God led me to do two things I thought I'd never do: forgive my earthly father and forgive my Heavenly Father. Unlike my earthly father, God had done nothing wrong that warranted forgiveness. Like a spoiled child, I believed that I deserved everything and that not even God had the right to snatch it all away. *"Shall we accept good from God, and not trouble?"* (Job 2:10 NIV) When my world was taken away, I accused God of making a mistake, being unjust and cruel. God showed me that I needed to repent of my pride and realize that His wisdom is above my wisdom. I should have noticed that God was trying to use my adversity to bring me closer to Him, but I was too busy judging Him to recognize the blessing. When I suffered, I should not have cursed God; instead, I should have asked for the wisdom to understand what I was going through, and the strength to get through it.

In my ignorance, I lived my life trying to find peace through my external circumstances. I think this is the number one mistake made by people who have suffered unexpected tragedy. Trying to heal ourselves through shortcuts like companionship, drugs, alcohol, and the list goes on. We think that if we'd just get our situation right again, we can be happy. But the truth is: if we are waiting on a perfect situation in order to be happy, happiness will never come. I had all the girls and lots of money, but had become more miserable each day. My pain and suffering caused me to lose hope in my future, and loss of hope in the future will eventually turn into a lack of power in the present.

I spent the last eight or nine years running on the treadmill of life. I was moving, using a lot of energy, but not going anywhere. Satan made me feel like it was God's fault that I lived in a sinful world where people were sick, suffering, and dying. It is not God's fault at all; it is ours. We had a world without pain and suffering, but Adam messed it up for everybody. So although God allowed my parents to die, it was not His fault. There is a difference.

God is not to blame for the fallen condition of our world, or the condition of the fallen people in it. God gives us rules to follow, but He does not make us follow them. When my dad chose to break the rules, God left him to suffer the consequences of his actions. Unfortunately, my mom died on behalf of his mistakes, which isn't fair, but it is life. I would be lying if I said that I fully understood it all, but I do understand that we have to deal with the impact that sin has on this world. When someone decides to drink and drive, they may hit your car. When someone decides to lie on a resume, they may get your job. When large banks get greedy, you may end up with a financial crisis. My dad made the decision to do wrong and ignore God; we all suffered for it.

In my immaturity I thought that what made God great was His ability to keep my life happy and free from adversity. But what truly makes God great is the strength He gives us to get through our adversity, and the ability He gives to turn it into good. God's strength will be made perfect in our weakness, if we don't turn our backs on Him.

I'd like to quote the mother of Len Bias, who was an All-American college basketball player, selected by the Boston Celtics as their second overall pick in the 1986 NBA Draft, but died two days later from cardiac arrhythmia induced by a cocaine overdose. He is considered by some sportswriters to be one of the greatest players not to play at the professional level. Two years after Len's death his younger brother was shot dead in a Maryland mall parking lot after walking away from an altercation. After the loss of two sons Len Bias' mother states in an ESPN 30 for 30 documentary,

"I know, to sit here and not be out of my mind, there is a God in heaven." This type of strength and faith can only come from the Lord God.

Instead of making God the bad guy during our adversity, we can choose now to make Him the purpose of our adversity. As one victim of misfortune prayed, "Tell me not why I must suffer, only assure me that I suffer for God's sake." I am convinced that my parents' deaths and my suffering will continue to bring God glory. I refuse to regret my adversity; this would be disrespectful to the legacies of my mother and father. No longer am I going to make my situation worse by making sinful decisions because I feel sorry for myself. God blessed me with a second chance, and I am going to make the best of it.

2010

I want to make the best of my second chance, not only for me, but also, for the very special people that God asked to sacrifice in order for me to have a second chance. People like the Harris' for their consistent love and friendship. I thank the whole Daniels, McKie, Gary, Carroll, Hardnett, and Settles families for being close, loving, and supportive family to Chantal and me through both deaths of our parents. To Fran Wygladalski, Claudette Noel, Chandra Ponder, Joyce Fleming, Ms. Kelly, Barbara McKormick and Linda Khein for being another set of loving motherly figures to me during the hardest times of my life.

To Charles and Carol, whom I now call Mom and Dad, for sacrificing life as they knew it to partake in our suffering. You both are the best! God has given me another father in Charles Daniels, who is the best role model a young man can have. His humble spirit, love, and dedication to his family motivate me each day to be a better husband and father. I have another mom who is my best friend, Carol Daniels. I have never met a sweeter, more compassionate woman. Her belief and confidence in me, when almost everyone else counted me out, is one of the biggest reasons that I am still here. My mother once told me that nobody would love me like she did, but I must say that despite her genius, this is one thing she got wrong. Carol's unconditional love is an exact match.

I must thank the entire U.S. Government for blessing me with a second chance. Though our government may not be perfect, it is better than any other, and deserves to be appreciated. To Sheila, who risked her livelihood to make sure I was given a second chance. She received lots of resistance from the ATF regarding my case, and pressure from her superiors to bring in a solid conviction, but she refused to let that prevent her from doing what God called her to do in my life. I am humbled and amazed by her love for me and her commitment to God. To ensure that Sheila's sacrifice was not made in vain, we continued to use our skills in a partnership to build our own mentor program, called Brother2 Brother. Sheila and I often talk about my story being the beginning of an extraordinary youth development program. We kicked off the Brother 2 Brother by recruiting volunteers and continuing to tutor, because studies indicate that there is a direct correlation between the reading level of African American fourth grade students and their odds of going to prison. People from our community donated buses to pick up the children and bring them to Sheila's house the last Saturday of each month for barbeque, basketball, football, go-carts, prayer, Bible reading and worship to God. When Sheila could no longer host the 200+ guests, we started using the church's facilities. Brother 2 Brother was eventually adopted as an official ministry at The Greenforest Baptist Church, and many of the children have given their lives to the Lord. God used my adversity to bring Sheila and me together in a partnership that will save thousands of lives.

I am convicted by my previous actions toward women. There were women in my life that trusted me, and I took advantage of their trust. I was wrong, and I'm very apologetic. I am also very sorry and pray that I will be forgiven by anyone who may have suffered in any capacity for any crime I, or anyone I was involved with, may have committed.

I am now drug and alcohol free, committed first and foremost to growing my relationship with Christ everyday that He wakes me up. I am a faithful husband to my beautiful wife, Linda (my sunshine) McKie, who, other than salvation, is the greatest gift God has given me. Without her, nothing I do would be remotely possible. Linda was the young lady I was dating, who my college professor advised not to continue seeing me because I'd end up in jail. I am so happy Linda didn't listen to her and saw something positive in me. We just had a beautiful daughter named Elyse last month. I am the proud father of a handsome and extremely bright 8 year old son name Jahlyn, who plays basketball, football and baseball. His mother is now happily married to a man who's an excellent second father to my son. I have been attending New Life Church in Lithonia, GA, for the last seven years, and my wife and I are proud members. I am the founder and C.E.O. of a Christian life coaching and counseling corporation named Real T.A.L.C. (Turning Around Life's Challenges). Despite my past and the economy, my God continues to provide exceedingly above all I could ever ask, think or deserve.

Chantal is a graduate of Spellman College, and is an excellent first grade teacher. I am the proud uncle to a bright six-year old nephew, DJ, and the cutest and bossiest three-year-old niece, Diane Carol, who was named after my two mothers. I'm the Godfather to the most loving two-year-old I have ever met, Charles Linden.

It has been seven full years since my sentencing day in December 2002, and I continue to learn more and more about my purpose each day. I write this, feeling much like I imagine Paul did when he said, "*I don't mean to say that I have already achieved these things or that I have already reached perfection. But I press on to possess that perfection for which Christ Jesus first possessed me. No, dear brothers and sisters, I have not achieved it, but I focus on this one thing: Forgetting the past and looking forward to what lies ahead.*" (Philippians 3:11-13 NLT) What lies ahead for me may not be a purpose of great fame or fortune, but a purpose that helps God establish an unwavering faith and trust in the hearts of His children. This type of purpose could have only been fulfilled by taking me through situations that were beyond my understanding and out of my control.

Dear brothers and sisters, *"when troubles come your way, consider it an opportunity for great joy. For you know that when your faith is tested, your endurance has a chance to grow. So let it grow, for when your endurance is fully developed, you will be perfect and complete, needing nothing."* (James 1:2-4 NLT) Like Christ, we all have been called to suffer for the sake of others. Pain and grace are not mutually exclusive. Without Christ's suffering, we, as sinners, could not receive grace, and without our own suffering for Christ others may not experience grace in certain areas of their life. God will show us how to use our suffering to lend a helping hand and protect others from the pain and suffering we went through.

We can not let Satan gain a foothold in our life by sowing seeds of anger and unforgivness. If we will ever overcome our adversity and bear fruits in our purpose we must stay connected to Christ. *"If a man remains in me and I in him, he will bear much fruit; apart from me you can do nothing."* (John 15:5 NIV) God is a master architect, and if we let Him, He will take our adversity and design a great purpose with it. I would not be where I am today, mentally or spiritually, if it were not for the difficulty I endured. And more importantly, there are many other people who wouldn't be where they are today, if it were not for my misfortune. *"If anyone would come after me, he must deny himself and take up his cross daily and follow me."* (Luke 9:23 NIV) Jesus Christ wants us to pick up our cross and follow Him so that He can teach us how to use our adversity to achieve God's purpose.

Interesting Facts: My mother died on December 23, and my second mother, Carol, was born on December 24. As we mourn the death of one mother, we celebrate the life of another. I often tease Carol by saying that the day after my mom died, my new mother was born. My sister's son's birthday is 12/02, and my son's birthday is 12/03. They merge together as 12/23, the date of my mother's death. I think this is God's unique way of reminding me that He has given me much more life than He allowed to be taken away.

PRAISE BE TO GOD!

Overcoming adversity and turning obstacles into stepping stones is the expertise of author, speaker, and philanthropist, Yannik McKie. At age 11 Yannik suffered the heartbreak of his parents' divorce and learned that both Mom and Dad were HIV positive. By the age of 15 Yannik lost both of his parents to the deadly AIDS disease. Overcoming such adversity has helped Yannik earn his reputation as an expert on how to overcome life's toughest challenges. Yannik's amazing life story has been featured on numerous media outlets including ESPN, The Huffington Post, The New York Daily News, Good Day Atlanta, and many more. Yannik is the Founder and Executive Director of the McKie Foundation through which he donates his time and resources to at-risk youth. For his efforts with youth, Yannik was awarded the Change Maker of the year award from the National Leadership Council and he was inducted into his alma mater, Georgia Southern University's, top 40 under 40 alumni class. Yannik's diverse life experiences make him a highly sought-after speaker for universities, businesses and nonprofit organizations. Yannik has a degree in marketing from Georgia Southern University and a Master's Degree in Christian Ministries from Liberty University. Yannik is the proud husband to his beautiful & supportive wife, Linda and the loving father to Jahlyn & Elyse McKie.

If you wish to stay informed about the McKie Foundation's current events please like, follow and subscribe to the McKie Foundations Facebook, Twitter and You Tube social network sites. Also, feel free to contact the McKie Foundation office at 1-800-827-3035, by email at inquiries@yannikmckie.com or through our website at yannikmckie.com.

experience as a source of knowledge, McKie has forged regimens for developing Biblically principled life skills and tools, meant to foster the sort of personal, social, and business life improvements so many are seeking, and not finding on their own.

Atlanta native, Yannik McKie's own challenging life experiences of losing both his parents to critical illness before the age of 15 served as mastery training ground; the hard won ability to turn tragedy and adversity into triumph and purpose, gives him the added impact of personal testimony and proven victory.

Professionally, McKie began his career in the health insurance business. By 2007 he had used his marketing and business savvy to progress through the ranks from recruiter, trainer, and manager of agents, to supervisor, team leader, and ultimately, to regional director in 2007, when he oversaw the business in 23 states. Among Atlanta, Georgia life and health insurance brokers, McKie was noted, as regional director, for accruing nearly $1 million in premiums during a twelve-month period.

Yannik used his skills to start his own business development and marketing firm in 2009. Yannik has worked with many corporations in the greater Atlanta area, like Atlanta Life & Health, Marketing Resources, and Marcy Gammon & Associates, just to name a few. Yannik was a leader in developing marketing strategies, constructing and analyzing marketing and advertising budgets to increase return on investment.

In 2010 Yannik began his newest business venture as an independent business owner of Real T.A.L.C. (Turning Around Life's Challenges). Yannik McKie offers motivational speaking services, as well as individual and group life coaching and counseling. Yannik is also the Executive Director of the MCKIE FOUNDATION, founded out of a family's commitment to help others in need of similar recovery, planning, and grace. For more information on Yannik's counseling, coaching and keynote speaking services please visit www.yannikmckie.com.

MCKIE FOUNDATION

MCKIE FOUNDATION

The McKie Foundation is a non-profit corporation committed to helping families in our communities turn their tragedies into triumphs.

"If it wasn't for the sacrifice of others,
I don't know where I would be today." **- Yannik McKie**

The MCKIE FOUNDATION includes six main initiatives:

1. Health and Wellness
2. STD Prevention

3. Philanthropy
4. At-risk Youth Development
5. Mentoring
6. Counseling

The McKie Foundation, also founded out of a family's commitment to help others in need of similar recovery, planning, and grace ... We believe that by positively affecting individuals in our communities we can change hearts, families, communities, and cities ... by changing cities, we can change states... states, the nation, the world.

> Remember them that are in bonds, as bound with them;
> and them which suffer adversity...**Hebrews 13:3 KJV**

We know you share our interest and dream of creating a higher standard of living for our community and its citizens. The McKie Foundation is a nonprofit and operates solely as funded by the generous support of tax deductible gifts from partners and friends. You can help us to change a life today not just with your financial support, but with any type of support you can provide. For more information on the MCKIE FOUNDATION and how you can partner with us please go to www.yannikmckie.com.

REFERENCES

Introduction

1. (Yancey, Phillip, Where is God When It Hurts, A Zondervan/Campus Life Publication, 95-97)
2. (Yancey, Phillip, Where is God When It Hurts, A Zondervan/Campus Life Publication, 97)

Chapter 1

1. (Peale, Norman, The Positive Power of Jesus Christ, Tyndale House Publishers, Inc., 15)

Chapter 4

2. (Avert.org)

Chapter 7

1. (Avert.org)

Chapter 8

3. (Kushner, Harold, When Bad Things Happen To Good People, Avon Books, 4)

Chapter 10

9. (Kushner, Harold, When Bad Things Happen To Good People, Avon Books, 68)

Chapter 11

4. (Kushner, Harold, When Bad Things Happen To Good People, Avon Books, 137)

Chapter 12

5. (Kushner, Harold, When Bad Things Happen To Good People, Avon Books, 38)
6. (Kushner, Harold, When Bad Things Happen To Good People, Avon Books, 38)

Chapter 18

10. (Norwood, Chris Yes America Has Aids Orphans—Lots April 7,2009)

Chapter 19

7. (IMDB.com)

Chapter 23

8. (Kushner, Harold, When Bad Things Happen To Good People, Avon Books, 139)

Made in the USA
Columbia, SC
17 January 2020